EXPLORE

C000172659

FUERTEVENTURA

Authors:
Bernd F. Gruschwitz,
Wolfgang Taschner

An Up-to-date travel guide
with 61 color photos
and 3 maps

NELLES

LEGEND / IMPRINT

Dear Reader: Being up-to-date is the main goal of the Nelles series. Our correspondents help keep us abreast of the latest developments in the travel scene, while our cartographers see to it that the maps are kept completely current. However, as the travel world is constantly changing, we cannot guarantee that all of the information contained in our books is always valid. Should you come across a discrepancy, please contact us at: Nelles Verlag, Schleißheimer Str. 371B, D-80935 Munich, Germany, tel: +(49) 89 35 71 940, fax: +(49) 89 35 71 94 30, e-mail: Nelles.Verlag@t-online.de.
Note: Distances and measurements, including temperatures, used in this guide are metric. For conversion information, please see the *Guidelines* section of this book.

LEGEND

★★	Main Attraction (on map)	
★★	(in text)	
★	Worth Seeing (on map)	
★	(in text)	
❽	Orientation Number in Text and on Map	
⊥	Lighthous	
♙	Castle	
☀	View Point	

Santa Cruz *(Town)* Places Highlighted
Iglesia *(Sight)* in Yellow Appear in Text

International/National Airport

Nature Reserve

Corona Mountain
(609) (altitude in meters)

\ 13 \ Distance in Kilometers

☀ Beach

∩ Cave

Principal Highway

Main Road

Provincial Road

Secondary Road

Car Ferry

Ⓢ Ⓢ Ⓢ Luxury Hotel Category
Ⓢ Ⓢ Moderate Hotel Category
Ⓢ Budget Hotel Category
(for price information see "Accomodation" in Guidelines section)

FUERTEVENTURA
© Nelles Verlag GmbH, 80935 München
All rights reserved

First Edition 2000
ISBN 3-88618-276-2 (Nelles Travel Pack)
ISBN 3-88618-774-8 (Nelles Pocket)
Printed in Slovenia

Publisher:	Günter Nelles	**Picture Editor:**	K. Bärmann-Thümmel
Managing Editor:	Berthold Schwarz	**Cartography:**	Nelles Verlag GmbH, Munich
English Edition Editor:	Rebekah Rollo		
Translation (partially):	Marita E. Döring, Kerstin Borch	**Lithos:**	Priegnitz, Munich
		Printing:	Gorenjski Tisk

TABLE OF CONTENTS

LIST OF MAPS

OCÉANO

ISLAS

LA PALMA

Pico de
la Cruz
(2351)
• Santa
Cruz

Los Llanos
de Aridane

TENERIFE

San Cristóbal
de la Laguna

Puerto de
la Cruz

SANTA CR

Pico del Teide
(3715)

Granadilla
de Abona

Los Cristianos

LA GOMERA

(1487)
San
Sebastián

— 28°

Valverde

EL HIERRO

Malpaso
(1501)

OCÉANO

18°

CANARY ISLANDS

0   50 km

14°

ATLÁNTICO

ALEGRANZA

MONTAÑA CLARA

GRACIOSA

CANARIAS
(SPAIN)

LANZAROTE

(608)

Arrecife

Playa Blanca

Corralejo

LOS LOBOS

FUERTEVENTURA

Puerto del Rosario

Betancuria
(724)

Gran Tarajal

Jandía
(807)

Moro del Jable

16

Gáldar

LAS PALMAS

Pico de las
Nieves
(1949)

GRAN CANARIA

Maspalomas

28°

ATLÁNTICO

Laayoune

MAROC

Lemsid

14°

7

The Island's Origins

Over 20 million years ago, after intense volcanic activity on the floor of the Atlantic Ocean, Fuerteventura surfaces as the second Canary Island, after Lanzarote.

Ca. 1100 B.C. The Phoenicians discover the Canary Islands. They are followed by the Carthaginians. However, after Carthage is destroyed by the Romans, the existence of the islands is all but forgotten.

Ca. 400 B.C. The Guanches, the first inhabitants of Gran Canaria – known as *Majoreros* in Spanish – begin to settle the islands. Today it is widely accepted that they were originally part of a nomadic Berber tribe that lived along the coast of North Africa, however, it remains unclear as to how they initially made their way to the islands.

The End of the Roman Era

Ca. 25 B.C. Rome sends Juba II, King of Numidia and Mauritania, and his navy to conquer the Canary Islands. They fail.

A.D. 100-160 Ptolemy draws the zero meridian through the Canary Island El Hierro, which, until the discovery of America, remains the westernmost point of the known world.

Into the Middle Ages the Guanches live in their Stone Age culture, undisturbed by outside influences; there is also practically no contact between the islands. While war and epidemics claim countless victims in Europe, the Guanches lead peaceful lives that are in harmony with nature.

The Conquest

1340-42 The Portuguese, Spanish and Mallorcans come to the Canary Islands to capture slaves.

1344 Luís de la Cerda, the great-grandson of King Alphonse X of Castile, is crowned king of the Canary Islands by Pope Clement VI. He dies, however, before he ever sets foot in his kingdom. At the same time, a Mallorcan map depicts an island known as *Forte Ventura* (meaning "Great Adventure" and/or "Strong Wind") located off the northwest coast of Africa.

1402 The Norman nobleman Jean de Béthencourt conquers Lanzarote.

1405 After receiving additional troops from Spain, Jean de Béthencourt is also able to defeat Fuerteventura. Maciot de Béthencourt is made viceroy of the islands.

1418 Count de Nibla buys the Canary Islands from Maciot de Béthencourt.

1430 Juan de las Casas buys himself the title to Fuerteventura.

1479 In the treaties of Alcáçovas and Toledo, Portugal gives control of the Canary Islands to Spain.

1492 Columbus uses the Canaries as the starting point for his first exploratory expedition. His future voyages (1493, 1498 and 1502) also begin here.

In the name of Castile, the Norman Jean de Béthencourt (1359-1425) conquered the Canary Islands of Lanzarote and Fuerteventura.

1496 Tenerife, the last independent bastion in the Canaries, falls under Spanish rule.

Under Spanish Rule

1500-54 Cultivation of sugar cane improves the economy, but the pace set by foreign competition can't be matched, and before long it largely disappears. Wood is used to fuel the sugar refineries and as a result large tracts of forest are destroyed.

16/17th Century The Canary Islands are repeatedly attacked by pirates from England, France, Holland and Portugal. For the first time in the history of the islands, economic hardship and water shortages cause many islanders to emigrate to Central and South America.

1708 A militia regiment is stationed in La Oliva, making it, for all practical purposes, the island's capital.

1730-36 Massive volcanic eruptions make a large portion of nearby Lanzarote uninhabitable.

The fort in El Cotillo, on the northwest coast of Fuerteventura, was built during the mid-18th century to protect against pirate attacks.

1740 In the Battle of Tamacite, two kilometers south of Tuineje, the *Majoreros* defeat a troop of English pirates who attacked the island (October 13, *Fiestas de San Miguel*). Soon after, defensive fortifications are built in El Cotillo and Caleta de Fustes.

19th Century Cultivation, and export as a dye, of the insect cochineal, which thrives on the cactus pears that grow in Fuerteventura's *malpaís* (badlands), revives the island's economy.

1834-35 Antigua is made the capital of Fuerteventura for a period of one year.

1835 Puerto de Cabras becomes the island's administrative capital.

1852 The Spanish Queen Isabella II declares the impoverished Canary Islands a free trade zone. The commercial trade and shipping industries thrive.

1880 Banana cultivation begins on the Canary Islands.

The 20th Century

Ca. 1910 The first windmills from America are delivered to Fuerteventura.

1912 Fuerteventura, like the other Canary Islands, is allowed to establish an Island Council *(Cabildo Insular)*, a self-administrating body.

1924 During the dictatorship of Primo de Rivera, the Basque educator, author and philosopher Miguel de Unamuno spends a few months of his exile on Fuerteventura. The Casa Museo Unamuno in Puerto de Rosario honors this man whose works reflect a great fondness for the island and its population.

1927 Las Palmas de Gran Canaria is made capital of the eastern island province, which includes Gran Canaria, Fuerteventura and Lanzarote.

1936 General Franco ushers in the beginning of the Spanish Civil War from the Canary Islands. After his victory he rules all of Spain from 1939-75.

1956 Puerto de Cabras is renamed Puerto del Rosario.

1966 Construction of the first vacation resorts begins on the Jandía Peninsula and in Corralejo.

1975 A portion of the Spanish Foreign Legion is transferred from the Sahara to Fuerteventura.

1978 Spain holds its first democratic elections.

1982 The Canary Islands are accorded the status of an autonomous region and are allowed to elect their first parliament.

1986 Spain enters the European Union. The Canary Islands remain a free trade zone.

1996 The foreign legion leaves Fuerteventura for the Spanish mainland.

Since 1997 the Spanish sculptor Eduardo Chillida has tried to get permission for a land-art project on the volcano Montaña de Tindaya. To date the project's opponents have thwarted his initiatives.

1999 The Canary Islands receive priority development status within the EU for another six years.

FUERTEVENTURA
Sun, Sand, Wind and Stars

Fuerteventura

PUERTO DEL ROSARIO
CORRALEJO AND THE NORTH
THE MIDWEST
THE SOUTH AND SOUTHEAST
THE JANDÍA PENINSULA

An Island Sahara

If you like broad expanses of desert and are naturally inclined towards meditation, you will appreciate the subtle changes of color that occur as sun and shadow dance across Fuerteventura's barren landscape. The ocher-colored volcanic stones practically glow in the light of the sunset, when the colors of the palm oases are even more intense usual, and among the sand dunes the contrast between sun and shadow is particularly pronounced. However, it isn't just the natural aesthetics of the volcanic cones, which have been smoothed and flattened by millions of years of erosion, that draw, year after year, vast numbers of tourists to Fuerteventura. It is the ocean, the broad sandy beaches and the golden yellow sand dunes that attract them – multitudes of sun-worshipers and an ever-increasing number of water-sport fans. (Water sports are very popular here, even though it is best not to swim outside the tourist areas because of the often fierce undertow.)

Previous Pages: The women of the Canary Islands are masters of hem-stitch embroidery. Playa del Moro – beach as far as the eye can see. The fascination of the volcanic desert in Fuerteventura's barren south. Left: A work of art in the harbor of Puerto del Rosario.

Fuerteventura either delights you or leaves you cold. It certainly isn't the "attractive holiday landscape" that many expect to find.

With all of the sand and rock that make up most of northern Fuerteventura's largely desolate landscape, it is rather reminiscent of the Sahara Desert. Apart from Maspalomas on Gran Canaria there is nowhere else in the Canary Islands with so many enormous dunes and sandy beaches. However, the one big difference to the Sahara is the ever-present reminders of the island's volcanic past – ever present despite the fact that the last volcanic activity to occur here was over 7000 years ago.

It is precisely because of its spacious and vast desert expanses that Fuerteventura takes some getting used to. At the beginning of the 20th century the Spanish government used Fuerteventura as a place of exile for unwanted politicians and intellectuals. Throughout the 1960s Spanish civil servants thought of a transfer to Fuerteventura as a form of punishment. In 1975/76 the Spanish government transferred its foreign legion from the Sahara to Puerto del Rosario. Thirty years ago no one could have believed that tourism would catch on upon this solitary island.

One of the island's exiles, Miguel de Unamuno, the poet and philosopher-dean of the University of Salamanca, was one of the people who initiated a change in the way people thought about Fuerteventura. During the time he spent here he was so charmed by the scenery and the warmth of the local population that he often included references to Fuerteventura in his later works. In Puerto del Rosario the Casa Museo Unamuno offers visitors a detailed look into Unamuno's life.

The island's ever-present beaches and prevailing winds attract large numbers of water sport enthusiasts to Fuerteventura. Surfers of every possible derivation, particularly windsurfers, feel right at home skimming across the water's surface, and divers and snorkelers happily frolic below the surface. Hikers, mountain bikers and motorcyclists love the wide-open landscape, and cyclists appreciate the well-paved roads. Most importantly, the miles and miles of sandy beaches in the south are ideal for families with children.

Arrival

The international **Aeropuerto del Rosario** is six kilometers to the south of Puerto del Rosario, and its new terminal hall is one of the most elegant anywhere in the Canary Islands. The airport contains numerous rental car companies, an information office (which also provides bus timetables and a broad array of informative brochures), an automatic teller machine and a currency exchange office. Keep in mind that because of more favorable exchange rates, it is better to exchange large sums of money in the bigger tourist resorts like Corralejo, Jandía Playa or Morro Jable.

If you are traveling as part of a package tour, you will be met by the tour operator's representative who will take take you to prearranged busses that are waiting to take you to your chosen destination. The drive to Corralejo or Morro Jable takes at least an hour, which will seem particularly long for those who are

OCÉANO

ATLÁNTIC

PENÍNSULA DE JANDÍA

Playa de Barlovento

Playa de Cofete
Punta   Jandí
Pesebre   Pico de la Zarza
                     Cofete   (80
Playa de   Parqu
Ojos   Las Talahijas
            (189)   Fraile
         Puerto   (683)   de
Faro de Jandía 30 de la Cruz
Punta de Jandía   Morro
                                     Jable
         Playa de las Pilas
Las Palmas   Playa de
                     Juan Gómez

OCÉANO ATLÁNTICO

FUERTEVENTURA

0   5   10   15 km

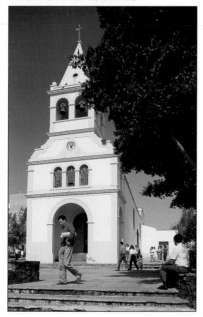

The more distant Canary Islands, including Tenerife, La Palma and El Hierro, can be reached either by a long water crossing with one of the car ferries or by plane. Several times a day the small planes belonging to *Binter Airlines* leave from the Aeropuerto del Rosario and make the short flights to the neighboring islands.

PUERTO DEL ROSARIO

From the airport a well-paved highway leads northwards to island's the capital of **Puerto del Rosario ❶** (pop. 19,000). To the south of the town is the rather monastically severe-looking **Parador Nacional de Fuerteventura**, with its latticed balcony (*azotea*), and the white sands of **Playa Blanca**, which is very popular with the local population. The Parador Nacional is the town's best hotel and is usually patronized by business travelers. Its restaurant is one of the best on the island and its typical Canarian décor and picturesque courtyard are well worth seeing.

traveling with small children. Because of this you might want to consider staying at the resort of Castillo de Fustes, which is just a few kilometers south of the airport and has child-friendly beaches.

Fuerteventura can also be reached by water. Once a day a speed boat crosses from Las Palmas de Gran Canaria to Morro Jable, and a car ferry lands in Puerto del Rosario several times a week. Crossing with the large ferries takes a lot longer than with the speed boats, but the fares are dramatically lower. It can also be reached directly from Lanzarote. You can either take the ferry, which crosses from Playa Blanca to Corralejo almost hourly durning the day, or you can take the large car ferry between the capitals of Arrecife and Puerto del Rosario (the crossing takes about three hours). Buses, taxis and rental cars for your continued journey are waiting at the harbor.

The simple *Puerto de Cabras* ("Goat Harbor") developed into an important port during the 19th century, largely because this is where the island's saltwort trade first began. Small, black rock-like clumps of soda ash were produced by burning the saltwort plant (*barrilla*), and this soda ash, or lime, was then used to make soap, particularly in England.

In 1860 the town was made the capital of Fuerteventura – as the successor to Betancuria, Antigua and La Oliva, all of them being located and protected further inland. It was only in 1956 that it was given the resonant name of Puerto del Rosario.

Despite its name, however, the town is not that attractive. Its harbor installations and the industrial area to the north tend to overshadow it quite a bit. And anyone who travels into town from Playa Blanca will pass the former red-light district of **Barrio Chino**, which is rather run-down

Above: The church Nuestra Señora in Puerto del Rosario. Right: Lucha canaria – a traditional sport that is very popular with the locals.

looking, as well as the other relics of the area's past industrialization: lime kilns which were fired by English coal until the beginning of the 20th century.

The harbor promenade has been rebuilt, and oversized sculptures of snails and seashells have given it an artistic edge. The main shopping street, **Avenida León y Castillo**, leads from the **Plaza de España** in the middle of the promenade into the less exciting town center.

There is, however, one highlight worth mentioning, on Calle Virgen del Rosario near the church: the former exile home of Miguel de Unamuno now houses the **Casa Museo Unamuno**, which contains several items that belonged to the poet, and reflects the atmosphere of the 1920s very well. Anyone who speaks Spanish will understand the numerous quotations of the poet that are arranged as mottoes in several of the rooms, and will be eager to read the forthcoming new edition of his *De Fuerteventura a Paris*.

Also located near the church you will find the roofed-over **Arena** for *lucha ca-naria*, Canarian-style wrestling, which is also used for major concert and dance events. The **Casa de la Cultura**, which is located on Calle Ramiro de Maeztu, regularly features exhibitions, plays and concerts as well.

Most of the area's visitors just take a brief stroll through this town before drinking a *café con leche* at Plaza de España, or at the square near the church, and leaving again. To make Puerto del Rosario more attractive to tourists, plans are afoot to turn the former red-light district into a tourist quarter and to transform the present foreign legion barracks area into a municipal park.

Anyone reasonably fit person who is traveling around here by bicycle can ride from Puerto del Rosario through the hilly interior of the island, via Antigua, Tuineje and Tarajalejo, as far as Jandía (see page 55). The traditional villages, valleys with palm trees and cacti, and several excellent views of the barren, gently sloping mountain ridges – or the spectacular panoramic stretch over Pájara then

through the lonely mountain and desert region as far as Istmo de la Pared, are worth the effort. If you prefer a little less exertion, take a leisurely ride northwards along the flat road from Puerto del Rosario and through the dunes as far as Corralejo, but you should keep in mind that on the out-bound portion of your trip you will be riding into the strong trade winds that constantly blow from the northeast.

CORRALEJO AND THE NORTH

The most important vacation center in northern Fuerteventura, Corralejo can be reached along the eastern coast road. The landscape here is noticeably barren and scarcely populated. About halfway through this desolation is the **Parque Holandés**, a half-completed vacation facility with an uncertain future; its aban-

Above: Horse rides at the Parque Holandés recreational facilities. Right: The sand dunes near Corralejo have been declared a wildlife park.

doned superstructures are easily recognizable even from a distance. The facility demonstrates that, despite growing numbers of tourists, it is still possible to make a bad investment. In this case it was Dutch investors – thus the name Parque Holandés – who weren't willing to throw good money after bad and instead just stopped construction after the first of the facility's completed hotels failed to draw the expected number of tourists. The most obvious reason for the lack of reservations is the fact that there isn't a beach anywhere nearby.

However, there are two good reasons not to give Parque Holandés the cold shoulder. One is the riding stable that offers everything a horse-lover could possibly dream of that has been established on the grounds. And the other is the relatively new **Centro Mirak**. Inside this spacious watery wonderland you will find a spring water swimming pool, a Finish and a chromotherapy sauna, a Turkish bath and a whirlpool, all of which are available throughout the day. There are

Fuerteventura

also opportunities for more relaxing activities, like a session in the Alpha Body Capsule, a full-body massage, or a hydromassage with algae.

Continuing towards Corralejo you will soon reach a broad and spectacular area of sand dunes. The dunes are in a protected area, as are the nearby kilometer-long beaches, and both are very popular with sunbathers and water-sport enthusiasts. In the **Parque Natural de las Dunas de Corralejo** ❷ isolation addicts can find just what they're looking for, even at the height of the tourist season. Equipped with water bottle, food and a hat (and remember there is no shade whatsoever around here), you can walk for miles through the fine, white sand, enjoy the grandiose view across the dunes, build a sandcastle, and wander around naked. Alongside the hardy, dry vegetation here you will find plenty of broken snail shells and the partially fossilized remains of a now extinct member of the bee family. The island's constant lack of water may have brought about the extinction of

these bees, but the wild goats that are generally nearby hardly seem to notice.

Even driving on the paved road along the dunes can be an impressive experience. The strong winds here regularly blow sand across the roads, and in extreme cases they must be cleared by a sand plow! Under no circumstances should you ever park your car outside the marked and paved parking lots – there is a distinct chance that it will get stuck in the sand.

Shortly before the dunes were declared a nature park, the two high-rise hotels of Tres Islas and Oliva Beach were quickly built in the white sand. Their small stores provide visitors with drinks, sunscreen and swimsuits, while chaise loungues and sunshades can be rented at a nearby section of beach. Small snack bars located near the hotels, and widely spread along the beach, also sell delicious food (seafood, shrimp cocktails), ice cream, beer and fruit juices.

A small train (the *Mini-Tren*) regularly plies between Corralejo and the dunes. If

you walk far enough along the dunes and away from the hotels, you can even enjoy a little nude sunbathing. If you are not a good swimmer make sure that you remember to be aware of the undertow, which can be quite strong at some sections of the beach. If you feel like taking a short walk after sunbathing, why not wander along the beach, between the sand and lava cliffs, back to Corralejo? There is a good view of the Isla de los Lobos, and you can end the day enjoying some delicious seafood in Corralejo.

Corralejo ❸ is an unpretentious and attractive vacation resort, and the town center has a real village feel to it. It is an international place, and unlike Costa Calma and Morro Jable, it is not overly British- or German-oriented. There is a pleasant mix of all kinds of vacationers here: surfers, unmarried mothers with curious children, shell collecting beach-

Above: The harbor promenade in Corralejos – a good place to relax. Right: Meeting point for souvenir hunters – the handicraft market.

combers, bikers with backpacks, and energetic retirees. There are smaller beaches south of the harbor, and the municipal beach next to the Hotel Hoplaco, located in the middle of subtropical gardens, is ideal for kids.

Avenida Generalísimo Franco, the busy main street, leads to the center and to the pedestrian zone.

In the **Centro Atlantico**, which is on this avenue, it is fiesta time every day of the year. Every evening groups of surfers gather here to celebrate and party late into the night in the area's various pubs.

The cozy **Plaza Felix Estvéez González**, which surrounded by restaurants, is a good place to eat outside, and every evening there is live music to accompany your meal. In the surrounding streets there are also several seafood restaurants, small boutiques and sports stores.

On the **Plaza Pública**, just on front of the tourist office, a **craft fair** has been established, offering Canary Island souvenirs and mass-produced African articles. If you are interested in German food and

sporting culture, nearby are two bars (next to each other) that serve German beer and *wurst*, and show German soccer games and Formula One races on their satellite TVs.

At carnival time, Corralejo, with all its processions and dancing, is the liveliest place on the island and if you are sensitive to noise don't make the mistake of booking accommodation in the town center during that time, because the music plays all night long.

A walking tour of the town almost always ends at the harbor where the boats to Isla de los Lobos and the ferries to nearby Lanzarote dock. There are a number of street cafés here that offer great views of the area's lively and colorful goings on.

Corralejo's town fathers and hotel keepers continue to eagerly and actively support expansion projects and every year new hotels and apartment complexes open their doors. The east side of town is one construction site after another, and even the areas that aren't slated for de-velopment until sometime in the future already have nicely paved roads running through them.

Corralejo is the perfect starting point for motorcycle, mountain bike or off-road excursions – all of which can be rented here without a problem. From town you can follow the rough northern coast trail to Majanicho, and from there you can head south to Lajares or west to El Cotillo. The 24-kilometer-long round-trip is perfect for a longer tour and all along the way you will discover plenty of wonderful opportunities to stop and rest and collect shells. Two of the more inviting places to stop are **Playa de Majanicho** and **Playa del Bacho de la Burra** on **Punta de la Tiñota**, the island's northern tip, where the windy conditions are perfect for windsurfing. Inviting though it may seem after being in the hot sun, swimming, is not recommend here because of the strong undertow.

Another great day trip is an excursion to explore the nearby **Isla de los Lobos**. Tickets can be obtained at the harbor and

in the pedestrian zone (the boat leaves in the morning and returns in the afternoon, the entire trip takes around 40 minutes and there are also organized tours). The boats arrive at **El Puertito**, a relatively deserted fishing village. The safest beach for swimming around here is **Playa de la Calera**, just a few minutes' walk away to the west, with a view of Fuerteventura. The island is an excellent place for swimming and walking tours (see page 50).

The vegetation on Isla de los Lobos, which is protected, is rather sparse and has adapted to the salty seawater. **Faro de Lobos**, an automatic lighthouse, stands at **Punta Martiño**, the northern tip. In the west, the 127-meter-high crater rim of **Montaña de Lobos** provides a good view of Lanzarote and Fuerteventura, and is the island's highest point. The waters

Above: Windsurfers off Isla de los Lobos. Right: The Torre de San Miguel, from the era of pirate attacks – today it is mostly friendly fishermen and vacationers that dock in El Cotillo's harbor.

near Faro de Lobos – especially the fish-rich straits of **El Río** with their steep reefs – are popular with divers and anglers.

Beach and Surfing Paradise

On your way to the northwest side of Fuerteventura you will start by traveling south, in the direction of La Oliva. Seven kilometers later you should turn off to the right, heading in the direction of Lajares. If you happen to like water sports, try taking a detour before you reach the turn-off and go to the surfing paradise near **Majanicho ④**, on the north coast. The winds here ensure that the surfing conditions are practically perfect year round, and the area is so popular with surfers that you won't have any problems finding yourself a board in nearby Lajares.

Lajares ⑤ is surrounded by a region of semi-desert that is made up of fallow fields. The entire plain is dotted with walls built to provide shelter from the wind. As recently as twenty years ago dromedaries were used to work the fields

in this region. Lajares itself is still home to traditional handicrafts such as the time-consuming *calados*, or hem-stitch embroidery. With great skill and patience the local women produce the most beautiful work. Lajares has two shops that sell their tablecloths, pottery and other craft products. However, since the younger generation is not very interested in learning such labor-intensive skills, the workshops are struggling to stay open and some of the skills may slip into obscurity.

If you follow signs to **Ermita de San Antonio de Padua** on the south side of town you will see two renovated windmills. One is the "male" *molino macho*, the older type that is familiar from *Don Quixote*. The second, a thinner "female" windmill, or *molina*, was developed by a miller from La Palma. Despite its simpler design it is more efficient (see page 49).

Another beach and surfing paradise is **El Cotillo ❻** on the northwest coast. The resort, which looks like it is only half-built, actually has a long history as a natural fishing harbor. It also exported its own

lime. During the economic recessions of previous centuries this is where countless ships filled with emigrants left for South and Central America. A new harbor with a massive quay wall is under currently construction here.

The old harbor, with its small bars and restaurants, is the most picturesque part of town. On the coast, slightly to the south, is the **Torre de San Miguel**, a guard tower that was built in 1743 to protect the old harbor. Ruined lime ovens can still be seen nearby. A footpath leads from here down to **Playa del Castillo**, one of the region's nicest beaches, located beneath a section of steep coastline.

Further to the south are the beaches of **Playa del Ajibe de la Cueva** and **Playa del Águila**, both of them are wild and remote; here you will find nothing but steely blue sky, dark blue ocean with white foam, and fine white sand. There are several sheltered places between the lava blocks for nude sunbathing. This place is perfect for surfers, but even if you are a good swimmer, you should only en-

ter the water if the water looks reasonably calm and you are aware of the possibility of a strong undertow.

North of El Cotillo is a large area of sand dunes with small sandy bays (*caletillas*) that are enclosed by lava cliffs. The housing estate of **Los Lagos** can be seen in the distance. The modern lighthouse, **Faro de Toston** on the north-western-most tip of the island, towers above the flat rocky bays with their beaches of fine white sand. Enthusiastic surfers can be seen in the waves here, and beachcombers will enjoy the varied vegetation as well as all of the fascinating marine life in the rock pools.

*La Oliva

The village of *La Oliva ❼, in the island's, interior was the political center of

Above: The parish church of La Olivia, former power center of Fuerteventura. Right: The picture gallery in the Centro de Arte Canario Case Mané.

Fuerteventura from the early 18th to mid-19th century, and some (renovated) buildings still survive from that time. In the center of town is the majestic white **Parroquiade Nuestra Señora de Candelaria** church, its square bell tower visible for miles around. The Renaissance portal has a finely-carved wooden door, and highlights inside include the *mudéjar* ceiling, a large painting of *The Last Judgment*, a baroque altar painting by Juan de Miranda (1723-1805) as well as some fine *trompe l'oeil* work.

Not far from the church, towards the northwest and along a small side road, the former tithe house **La Cilla** contains a small exhibition of framing tools. In the eastern part of town is the semi-renovated townhouse **Casa de los Coroneles**. It is the largest historical structure of its type in the entire Canary Islands. This was where the island's military governors – the family of Cabrera-Béthencourt, descended from the Norman Jean de Béthencourt – used to reside. The family's coat of arms located above the portal

is worth noting, as are the artistically-carved wooden balustrades on the front balconies, and the square corner towers. A cultural center is due to be opened here in the near future.

Separated from the Casa de los Coroneles by a square, and to the northwest, is the **Casa del Capellán**, which is initially rather inconspicuous. The stonemasonry on the door and window frames of this former presbytery indicates the Latin American, and particularly Cuban, influence that was brought back to the islands by returning emigrants.

Lovers of Canarian modern art will appreciate the ***Centro de Arte Canario Casa Mané**, which is located between the church and the Casa de los Coroneles. On the ground floor it has rooms for current exhibitions and the basement contains a large contemporary art gallery. Outside there is a sculpture courtyard. Even if your taste in art runs more toward the conservative you should take a few minutes to look around. Not everything here is modern – some of the landscapes

by Agulló, for instance, are rather traditional.

From La Oliva the main road carries on towards the south, while a well-paved road branches westwards to **Tindaya ⑧**, at the base of the volcano of the same name, **Montaña de Tindaya** (401 meters). On this reddish-brown mountain, which was sacred to the Guanches, the islands' original inhabitants, a number of stylized footprints were recently discovered carved into the rock; their origin is still a mystery. Some assume that a cultic site was once located on the summit, especially since Tenerife's Pico del Teide, the Canary Islands' equivalent of Mount Fujiyama, is clearly visible from there.

A proposed project by the Spanish sculptor Eduardo Chillida (born in 1924) is causing a lot of controversy: he wants to carve a cube, with 50-meter-long sides, out of the center of the mountain. It will be lit from above by two shafts and standing inside, visitors are supposed to feel like "funny little gnomes" because of its giant dimensions. The locals hope it will

attract tourists and bring them more income than what they currently earn selling tomatoes and cheese. However, its opponents are still fighting and it could be quite a while before a decision is made.

A narrow asphalt road – which later becomes nothing more than a trail – leads from Tindaya to the west coast and the remote little **Playa de Janubio**, which is surrounded by sand dunes. This is a good place to get away from it all, but be careful of the undertow if you go swimming!

South of Tindaya, on **Montaña Quemada** (294 meters), the **Monumento a Don Miguel de Unamuno** was erected in 1970 in honor of the illustrious exile. The slightly larger-than-life-size statue of the poet-philosopher was only officially "opened" after the death of Generalísimo Franco because of fears that the regime would take offense to it.

Above: Along the way from La Matilla to Tefía.
Right: Windmills are a striking feature of the barren landscape (here near Llanos de la Concepción.

The main road leads to the southeast, via the villages of La Matilla and Tetir, to Puerto Rosario. However, if you turn sharply south just before La Matilla you will arrive in **Tefía ❾**. On the southern edge of the village various old farmhouses and windmills have been renovated using European Union funds. These pretty houses will provide the area's traditional arts and crafts with a new home in the near future.

Take a detour to the west coast and after a while you will pass another renovated windmill. Shortly after the small settlement of Las Parcelas, the road leads on to the Barranco de los Molinos. Nearby is the simple harbor village of **Los Molinos ❿**. It has a pond with geese and a pleasantly atmospheric little restaurant with a view of the rocks and surf.

THROUGH THE "MIDWEST"

From Tefía, the well-paved road continues on its way further southwards. At a traffic circle follow the signs to "Betan-

Fuerteventura

curia" off to the right (that is to say, to the west). Near **Llanos de la Concepción** there is a windmill up on a slope. From here you can get to the west coast, with its dark basalt cliffs, and **Aguas Verdes ⓫**, a remote vacation club located on **Playa del Valle**. Since 1984, the surf here has been smashing against a rusty old wreck – a formerly 100-meter-long freighter that was washed ashore. It is still possible to enjoy a quiet and relaxing vacation here, but swimming is only allowed in a few protected areas because of the strong undertow that is found along almost all of the west coast.

Further to the north are **Playa de Santa Inés** and **Playa de los Mozos**. Footpaths lead northwards along the coast to Los Molinos, southwards to Ajuy, or back through a *barranco* to Llanos de la Concepción. On all of these hikes you can remain almost completely undisturbed for the entire day. This relative isolation makes it all the more important to take the proper equipment along. You should have sturdy shoes, plenty of sunscreen and a hat, something to eat and, of course, lots of water.

From Llanos de la Concepción the road winds its way through the fertile and partially terraced **Valle de Santa Inés**, then onwards into the central hills. Along the side of the road you can see the terraced fields and agricultural areas that are typical of the Canaries. Just before Betancuria, at the next fork in the road, keep to the right (going west) and you will reach the toll road that leads up to the 645-meter-high **Tegú**, with its new ***Mirador Morro Velosa**. From this observation point – and from its telescope – you have an astonishing view of the entire northern part of the island. It is also clear how much of the island's surface has been eroded by climatic influences. Below the lush irrigated fields lie in strong contrast with their barren brown surroundings. In good conditions you can even see the neighboring island of Gran Canaria on the western horizon. The restaurant, which was co-designed by Blanca Cabrera, César Manrique's niece, is an ideal

place for a meal, and the giant windows allow you to enjoy the magnificent view from inside.

*Betancuria – the First Capital

The journey then continues down into the valley and to ***Betancuria 12**, which was founded by Norman conqueror Jean de Béthencourt in 1405 and remained the capital of the island until 1835. The whole town is a protected site, and its buildings are still thoroughly medieval-looking. Just outside the town is a renovated monastery, the **Convento de San Buenaventura**, which was erected by Franciscans after the *Conquista*; its outer walls, columns and archways are still standing. After secularization in 1836, the building was left to go to ruin, and many stones were used as building mate-

Above: Irrigation is still important in Betancuria, despite its high elevation. Right: The fortified church in Betancuria, the former capital, is now a museum.

rial. The badly-weathered tomb slab of the conqueror Diego García de Herrera, who died in 1485, remains, as does the intact but usually closed **Capilla de San Diego de Alcalá**, built above the cave of Franciscan hermit San Diego de Alcalá.

In the town center is the three-aisled **Iglesia Nuestra Señora de la Concepción** (Calle Alcaldo Carmelo Silvera), which was originally built around 1620 as a fortified church and today is a museum. The *mudéjar* ceiling is particularly fine, as are the Baroque high altar dating from 1684, with magnificent colors and fruit motifs, and the choir stalls, separated from the rest of the interior by a painted rood screen. The entrance fee to the church also includes access to the **Museo de Arte Sacro**, in an old townhouse behind the church. The various religious relics on display here include a section of material from the original banner of conquest that the King of Castile presented to his vassal Diego García Herrera.

The attractively restored **Casa Santa María** (16th century), near the church square, is an elegant place to enjoy a good meal. Take a few minutes to walk around the rooms and inner courtyards; it is really atmospheric. The ceramic and local handicraft shop in the basement is also well worth a visit.

On the main street, the **Casa Museo Arqueológico de Betancuria**, flanked by cannon, contains a collection of important and fascinating archeological finds. Highlights here include fertility idols, an idol frieze that was discovered near La Oliva, and numerous farming implements. The **Centro Insular de Artesania**, next to the museum, documents traditional arts and crafts.

Five and a half kilometers south of Betancuria, a road to the west leads to a valley of palm trees and the simple village of **Vega de Río de las Palmas 13**, nestled amid fields that are still largely cultivated. On its main street is the region's second most important church, after the one in

Betancuria, the **Iglesia Nuestra Señora de la Peña** (17th century). It contains a *Madonna and Child* made of alabaster that was apparently brought to the island from Normandy by Jean de Béthencourt, and was originally in the church in Betancuria. Hidden away during a pirate raid, the alabaster figure was thought to have been lost for good. Apparently it was rediscovered inside a cave west of Vega de Río de las Palmas – near the banks of a modern reservoir. Today the **Ermita de la Peña** marks the site where it was found. And this is why it is housed here instead of Betancuria.

The *Virgen de la Peña*, the island's patron saint, is believed to bring rain for the crops, and a major pilgrimage to Vega de Río de las Palmas takes place every year in September.

At the end of the valley is a large embankment and reservoir dating from the Franco period. In addition to collecting rainwater, it also collected great masses of mud, which means today it has almost completely filled with sediment. The shallow water, which once attracted large flocks of waterfowl and other birds, reportedly even a few flamingoes, no longer does so.

Pájara and Environs

The main road now winds its way around numerous hairpin bends as it ascends the **Fénduca** (609 meters, with an observation point at the top) and then continues on to Pájara – rock on one side, a massively steep drop on the other, and very few places for vehicles to pass. Luckily, solid walls line the outside edge to prevent anyone from falling to their death. The remote terrain is very impressive, especially in the spring when the green plants contrast sharply with the dark rock and shadows of the mountains.

Quiet little **Pájara** ⓮, with a population of around 700, has the only freshwater swimming pool on the island. The townspeople are thinking of expanding, but so far they have, fortunately, had no real idea of how to should do so. The

leafy church square and the parks are still idyllic, and there is also a fine old disused waterwheel outside the town hall that was once driven by dromedaries – whose job today is to carry tourists around. The town's many restaurants with good local menus invite you to take a break.

Pájara has one building that is definitely worth visiting, all the more so because of its Latin American elements: the **Iglesia Nuestra Señora de la Regla** (built between 1687 and 1711) in the center is quite striking with its extremely fine portico. The stonework here, with all its floral geometrical patterns, clearly betrays Latin American influence. The church is named after the patron saint of Havana, Cuba, and the Virgin at the central altar is thought to have been brought to Fuerteventura by a wealthy emigrant returning from Cuba.

Above: Strikingly South American – the ornamental façade of the church Nuestra Señora de la Regla in Pájara. Right: Steep coastline near Ajuy.

From Pájara there you can take a detour to **Ajuy** ⓯ on the west coast, a fishing village still largely untouched by tourism. It has two restaurants on its pebble beach and accommodation is provided by local boarding houses. A pleasant walking path leads from the sandy black beach northwards along the steep coast to Ajuy's **old harbor**. A layer of limestone has risen from the water here, and has some fine natural formations along it.

A flight of steps has been hewn out of the rock a little further north and they provide access to the bay of Caleta Negra, with its two enormous caves (see page 53). The first one ends when the sea breaks through after about 150 meters, while the second is longer and darker, so bring a powerful flashlight if you plan to do some exploring – and don't go inside if the surf is up.

On the trip back to Pájara there is a worthwhile detour (turn to the left after two kilometers) to **Barranco de la Madre del Agua**, a palm valley with a little

stream that has formed a number of pools – the perfect place to stop and unwind.

The road from Pájara to the Jandía Peninsula passes through a thinly populated mountainous region with very little vegetation. Much of the area towards the west has been sealed off and is used by the military. The high peaks of **La Tablada** (619 meters) and **Montaña Cardón** (691 meters) can be seen, occasionally encircled by clouds. A few crows are the only signs of life in this inhospitable area.

La Pared ⓰, where the road again reaches the coast, is a fashionable development with a vacation center, golf academy and luxury hotel and an incredibly kitschy avenue. The only reasonably remote place around here is **Playa del Viejo Rey** to the south, on a wild section of rocky coastline.

The name *La Pared* ("The Wall") refers to a land wall that apparently separated the Jandía Peninsula from the rest of Fuerteventura during time of the Guanches. Béthencourt's chroniclers refer to it as the wall separating the two kingdoms

of Maxorata and Jandía. In 1983, a construction company apparently used it as an illegal quarry. Today very little remains but a few rocks at the northern end.

Crossing the **Istmo de la Pared** in a southerly direction, you will get your first look at the sand and dune landscape of the Jandía Peninsula. The vegetation here is typical for Fuerteventura and consists mainly of a weed known as *aulaga majorera*, or prickly lettuce.

If you feel like exploring more of the interior from Pájara, you can take the scenic route to **Tuineje** ⓱, via **Toto**. Although the town is the center of a *Municipio*, it is still a very sleepy place. However, things were very different in 1740, when 37 farmers – armed with five muskets and various bizarre agricultural implements – hurried here to fight a troop of 50 English pirates that had arrived with guns and cannon. On **Montaña de Tamacite** (346 meters) to the south, the farmers actually won by advancing behind their field dromedaries. They waited behind their animals for the first salvo

from the English, then charged before the enemy had time to reload. Thirty Englishmen and five *Majoreros* (the name Fuerteventurans have given themselves) were killed that day. Two of the captured cannon can still be seen in front of the museum in Betancuria.

The historic incident has also been immortalized in a painting at the foot of the altar in the 18th-century **Iglesia de San Miguel Árcangel**, and a colorful "battle" is still the highlight of annual fiesta (late September/early October).

In the neighboring village of **Tiscamanita ⑱**, in the **Centro de Interpretación de los Molinos**, you can find exhibits and literature about the island's once widespread windmill-culture. In addition to a restored windmill there are also exhibits that document the daily life and work of a miller.

Above: Live guitar music in the bar Artesana – every form of Canary culture is preserved in Antigua. Right: The chapel of La Ampuyenta with all its fascinating frescoes and paintings.

Antigua – Center of Art

Antigua ⑲ was the island's capital – for one year – during 1835. Located in a fertile valley and founded in 1485, it is the island's cultural center. At the entrance to the town you can see modern art in the form of iron sculptures. An annual folklore convention and a large craft market (second Sunday of the month, 10 a.m. to 4 p.m.) underline the Antigua's creative role.

The single-aisled **Iglesia Nuestra Señora de Antigua** (1785) in the town's center has a *mudéjar* ceiling and a painting of the Last Judgment. While other churches display depictions of Hell, Antigua's the believers have been spared its horrors. The retable on the right-hand wall is a stone relief.

Leave the town center heading north and you come to one of the island's finer new creations, up on a windswept rise – a renovated windmill is surrounded by the museum village known as **Molino de Antigua**. Built under the supervision of

César Manrique, there are exhibition halls on art, history and archeology, a restaurant (usually fully booked) where cookery students can practice on the guests, studios for artists and craftsmen, a craft goods shop, a cactus garden and a conference hall. To some visitors, however, the whole place jars slightly with the more practical, down-to-earth reality of Fuerteventura as a whole.

There is a real artistic jewel five kilometers to the north in **La Ampuyenta ⑳**. Behind a conspicuous hospital building (1891) that was never used, is the carefully renovated little ***Iglesia de San Pedro de Alcántara**, the interior of which is packed with frescoes and paintings. Even the pulpit is covered with them. Nowhere else on the island is there such rich and diverse art, and the monumental paintings on the walls on both sides of the transept are breathtaking. The cycle of paintings shows episodes from the life of San Pedro. It is assumed that Juan de Miranda (1723-1805), from Gran Canaria, was the artist responsible for

these, and for the baroque *trompe l'oeil* work near the altar. This is one place you should certainly spend some time: the longer you look at the frescoes and paintings, the more astonishing it is that they could have been created in the first place.

After a quick stop in **Casillas del Ángel ㉑**, with its baroque **Iglesia de Santa Ana** (1781, dark lava facade), the journey continues on back to Puerto del Rosario.

THE SOUTH AND SOUTHEAST
Beaches and Fishing Villages

The coast road leads southwards from the capital, past the airport. Seven kilometers later **El Castillo**, also known as **Caleta de Fustes ㉒**, can be seen on a broad bay. This resort village with its sandy white beach is considered to be exemplary: there are no ugly hotel tower blocks, and accommodation is provided in bungalows built in the Moorish-Canarian style. The landmark of this small planned community with over 10,000 beds is the domed tower of the harbor

building near the marina, which houses the *Puerto Castillo* restaurant, a bar and a disco. There is a wonderful view of the whole town from its rooftop terrace.

Playa del Castillo is ideal for families with children, with its calm sea and clean water (see page 68). The harbor quay protects against the surf, so this is a good place to learn the rudimentaries of windsurfing without being repeatedly blown over. There are also good restaurants and boutiques here, and countless opportunities for sporting activities like sailing and diving, as well as a variety of excursions with boats, mountain bikes or motorcycles.

Cyclists and pedestrians will enjoy a trip southwards along the coast to the saltworks of **Las Salinas** (three kilometers), which is being funded by the European Union as an open-air museum. The ancient remains of a Guanch settlement were discovered in the **Barranco de la Torre**, south of Las Salinas.

The coast road turns inland at Las Salinas (the camel herds that you can see off to the right after about five kilometers area great distraction for the kids) and the region soon turns into inhospitable *malpais* (badlands) where a solidified river of molten lava has made the terrain uncultivable. On the left, a narrow street leads through a *barranco* towards the sea, and the little fishing village of **Pozo Negro** ㉓. The name means "black well," and the village is primarily visited on the weekends, when simple, but delicious seafood is served in the local restaurants. **Playa Pozo Negro**, with its dark sand, is dotted with colorful fishing boats and nets, but it isn't a very good place to go swimming.

Back on the main road you will cross the *Malpaís Grande* until you reach a major intersection. A short distance away, in the direction of Gran Tarajal, is the **Quesería Maxorata** dairy, where you can buy

Above: A favorite with families and those who are new to water sports – Playa del Castillo. Right: Trucks and jeeps are perfectly suited for exploring the island's interior.

Fuerteventura

delicious goat's cheese. Following the traditional, labor-intensive process, the cheese is still made by hand. The process begins with the milking of the goats, after which the milk is heated and the whey and curd are separated. The curd is then pressed, by hand, into forms, a job that is almost always by women. The goats' diet, the quality of the milk, and where the cheese is made and stored all work in unison to create the unique flavor of the *Queso Majorero*.

It takes the daily milk production of 90 goats to make just 15 kilograms of goat's cheese, which tastes best when it is fresh (*fresco*), but you can also try soft (*tierno*), half-cured (*semicurado*), ripe (*curado*) and aged (*viejo*) variations.

Heading south, travel a short distance towards the harbor town of Gran Tarajal, and just before you get there turn to the left, heading to the village of **Las Playitas** ㉔. This is one of the finest coastal villages on all of Fuerteventura. Its cube-like white buildings line the coastal slope, giving the whole place a very Moorish

feel. Many wealthy Canarios have their second homes here. At the entrance to the village is a dark sandy beach, and there is one with lighter sand a few meters west of the village center. Fishing boats bring in their catches during the afternoon, and the fish is served soon after in the seafood restaurant on the promenade. Even if your vacation package includes all of your meals, you should skip one and try, in this comfortable location, the grilled fish (*a la plancha*) with the inevitable boiled potatoes with a spicy sauce (*papas arrugadas con mojo*) and a glass of wine.

A detour to the east leads along a narrow paved road to the **Punta de la Entallada**. There, roughly 200 meters above the sea, is a massive fortress-like lighthouse (closed to the public). From the parking lot in front of it you can get a good view of the impressive rocky coastline here.

Gran Tarajal ㉕ is the second-largest town on the island, and it owes its growth to the brief heyday that was enjoyed by its harbor: it was from here that the island's

tomatoes were once shipped. Today they are exported from Puerto del Rosario. Local kids play soccer on the dark beach, and surfers can be seen riding the waves on their plastic boards. In the evening he beach promenade fills up for the *paseo*, and small shops in the narrow streets set the tone for shopping.

Gran Tarajal isn't trying to be anything special – and this lack of pretension makes it far more authentic than most of the island's coastal towns, but despite its authenticity, tourists very rarely stray here. One highlight of the town's center is the fountain with its water-spouting sea horses. The church beside it was built in the 20th century, its construction financed by an emigrant returning from Cuba, who also introduced metal wind wheels to the island.

Above: Powered by the wind – on Fuerteventura wind is a constant source of energy. (Parque Eólico near Costa Calma). Right: There are miles of sandy beaches on the Jandía Peninsula.

Tarajalejo ㉖ is a strange blend of fishing village and tourist center. Simple, attractively whitewashed and highly picturesque fishermen's houses in narrow alleys are as much a part of the scenery here as modern supermarkets, expensive boutiques, galleries and the large Club Hotel Tofio with its riding school. Its beach, covered with imported yellow sand, however, isn't quite as pleasant as those that are further south.

On the way to the Jandía Peninsula it is worth stopping at the **Zoo Parque de los Camellos**, near **La Lajita** ㉗. As well as the apes and birds, the island's flora also takes center stage here. But for kids, the best part is the parrot shows, which can be seen several times daily. Across the street from the zoo, ponies and dromedaries wait for curious tourists. In addition to a short ride around the surrounding area, it is also possible to take a longer excursion down to the beach where you can enjoy swimming and a picnic.

The houses on the coast are inhabited by fishermen and commuters who work in the tourism business on Jandía. Although apartment buildings have been here for quite some time, the beach still smells far more of sea and fish rather than of coconut suntan oil. Fishermen can often be seen mending their nets, and the marks of the boats in the sand make it clear that they are used on a daily basis.

THE JANDÍA PENINSULA

The long southwestern end of Fuerteventura, with its broad beaches, desert-like sand-dune landscapes and wild, rocky coasts, was made into a nature reserve in 1987, the **Parque Natural de Jandía**. The first large settlement west of the Istmo de la Pared is **Costa Calma** ㉘. Its infrastructure is largely tailored towards German-speaking visitors. The vacation area lies on either side of the much-traveled road, surrounded by parks with luxuriant foliage and flowers. Most

hotels offer a broad range of sports and entertainment activities, including beach parties, and there are restaurants and bars for the evenings – though it must be said that the standards of cuisine here are generally lower than they are elsewhere on the island.

The highlight of Costa Calma is to the southwest – the kilometer-long sandy beach of **Playa Barca**. It has remarkably clean waters and amazingly, it is easy to find a quiet, sheltered spot here even during peak season. Windsurfers are particularly fond of this beach.

If you continue in a southerly direction you will see the modern wind-power station of **Parque Eólico de Cañada de Río Costa Calma**. A total of 45 modern wind wheels rotate in the constant wind and they generated almost 14 percent of Fuerteventura's electric energy. During the windy months of July and August the station, which was built in 1993 with an investment of over ten million dollars, can produce up to an amazing seven gigawatt-hours of energy.

**Playas de Sotavento de Jandía extends for around 20 kilometers from here, with spectacular golden beaches, sand dunes and sparkling lagoons. *Sotavento* means "turned away from the wind" – the wind usually blows away from the land and out across the water. And it is because of the winds that this area has become a windsurfer's paradise – every year a world cup competition that draws the world's best windsurfers is held here. There are several tourist-friendly surfer shops that rent boards and offer classes (see page 64).

The highlight here is the endless beach near the two large dunes of ***Risco del Paso**, with several lagoons and a sandy promontory. Families with kids really appreciate the beach's clear waters and relatively calm sea. The windsurfers' colorful sails and the white crests of the waves further accentuate the multiplicity of greenish-blue tones. If you follow the signs to the nearby **mirador** and you can easily photograph this miniature and colorful paradise.

Jandía Playa and Morro Jable

The tourism industry is back in full swing at **Jandía Playa ㉙**. Holiday clubs, hotels, bungalows, shopping centers, restaurants, bars and discotheques can be found all over Fuerteventura's largest vacation center. There are some emptyish beaches around here, too, however, like the almost 50-meter-wide beach of fine sand at **Playa del Matorral** between Jandía and Morro Jable, which has the odd secluded spot along its edges.

Most of the tourists here are German, and during the day water sports, beach volleyball and beach gymnastics are all very popular. Individualists tend to ride off on bicycle or motorcycle tours of the surrounding area.

In the evenings Jandía Playa, with its lively restaurants, discos, bars and pubs,

Above: Paella, the Spanish national dish, is a culinary hit on the beach. Right: A modern wind wheel is the largest landmark in Puerto de la Cruz.

is one of the most happening places on this otherwise rather sleepy island.

The holiday center of **Morro Jable**, which developed from actual town, is located nearby. From Jandía Playa a nicely paved footpath follows the beach to Morro Jable, and around sunset it is usually filled with tourists who are taking one last walk for the day. Naturally the old fishing infrastructure has long since been superseded by hotels, and the nearby hillsides are covered with buildings, but when the town's old men play their guitars and timples on the promenade during the evenings, you still get a sense of old Canarian life.

Still further to the west, just behind the harbor where the speed boat from Las Palmas de Gran Canaria docks every day, is a dusty washboard track that leads 20 kilometers across inhospitable terrain to **Punta de Jandía**. With a four-wheel-drive vehicle or on a mountain bike (preferably one with shocks) – both can be rented in Morro Jable – this can make a very interesting day trip.

After just a few kilometers you can see, on the mountainside to the right of the road, several examples of the endemic Jandía wolf's-milk (*Euphorbia handiensis*), with its thick arms and long spines. A little further on the road passes Casas de Jorós. In the surrounding area, from January to April, giant gray tarps protect the tomato crop.

Ten kilometers further along there is a left-hand turn to **Playa de Juan Gómez**, with its attractive mixture of black and golden sand, plus a path that leads off to the equally attractive **Playa de las Pilas**, which is just a little further on.

The last place of habitation in western Fuerteventura is the godforsaken town of **Puerto de la Cruz 30**, nestling in the shadow of a modern wind-power station. A bar and a restaurant provide visitors – most of them traveling there in four-wheel-drive vehicles – with refreshment. The atmosphere and setting of the whole place is reminiscent of an American road movie. Out at the Punta de Jandía itself, there is a lighthouse.

The striking **Punta Pesebre** can be reached along a narrow paved road and in good conditions there is a great view of the coastline from here. There is also a good hike along a stony path to the 189-meter-high mountain – or rather hill – of **Las Talahijas**.

On the way back towards Morro Jable a turnoff near Las Pilas leads north to a 400-meter-high pass. There is a very windy **mirador** up here, but if you can withstand the gusts you will greatly enjoy the view across the north coast of the Jandía Peninsula and the sandy beach of **Playa de Cofete**, with the 12-kilometer-long **Playa de Barlovento** to east of it. *Barlovento* means that the wind blows from the sea across the land.

Cofete 31, which consists of just a few houses and makeshift shacks, and a small bar with a terrace, is another seemingly godforsaken place.

The many goats that jump and spring around the area around Cofete are rather conspicuous. Many of them are half wild, which means that they roam freely, but a

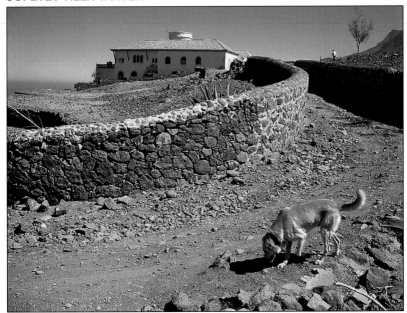

Above: The mysterious Villa Winter.

shepherd is never far away. They are milked every evening and are kept in stalls overnight. The completely wild goats (*cabras de costa*), on the other hand, which, to the horror of environmentalists, eat the few plants that the barren soil produces, are rounded up only once a year, during the *Apañada*, which sees the locals, with the help of their *bardinos* (sheep dogs), drive the goats into a *gambuesa* (pen). Once they are penned, the old and sick animals are separated, the young ones are marked, and the rest are set free. The *Apañada* is the highpoint of the year and is celebrated with great festivities.

The nearby **Villa Winter**, beneath the 807-meter-high **Pico de la Zarza**, Fuerteventura's highest peak, belongs to the descendants of a mysterious German named Gustav Winter, who enjoyed the protection of Franco during the latter's regime.

Some say that it was from this villa that Winter ran a secret submarine base for the German navy during World War II. Considering the German activities in northern Aftrica, this tactical location in southwestern Fuerteventura could have been very important. The locals often talk about a secret underground tunnel that runs from the villa down to the sea, which is rumored to have been used by important Nazis who were fleeing at the end of the war. They supposedly hid here, then took a boat on to South America. In other places it has been written that Gustav Winter planned to open a fish processing plant in Morro Jable, so he could take advantage of rich fishing grounds off of Africa's west coast.

Whatever the case, the precariously exposed location of the villa, which has been empty for decades and is starting to look rather dilapidated, gives rise to a lot of speculation.

By the way, if you feel like taking a swim at this point, to relax and recover from the strains of your journey, don't – the undertow is exceptionally dangerous and unpredictable.

FUERTEVENTURA

ARRIVAL: **By Plane**: *Aeropuerto del Rosario*, 6 kilometers south of Puerto del Rosario, tel: 928 851 250. Rental cars, cash machines and currency exchange. Inter-island flights: *Binter*, tel: 928 860 511.

By Boat: *Naviera Armas* shipping company, Puerto del Rosario, tel: 928 851 542 and 928 531 560. Speedboat *Jetfoil*, Las Palmas de Gran Canaria to Morro Jable (1.5 hours). Car ferry, Gran Canaria to Puerto del Rosario (8 hours). Lanzarote (Playa Blanca) to Corralejo (30 minutes). Arrecife to Puerto del Rosario (3 hours). **Bus**: The bus network, which is run by the *Tiadhe* company, connects the larger towns on the island.

i Kiosk in the airport, information about accommodation, transportation and sights, tel: 928 860 500.

THE NORTHEAST

PUERTO DEL ROSARIO

Parador Nacional de Fuerteventura, Playa Blanca 45, tel: 928 851 150, fax: 928 851 158. Colonial-style, excellent restaurant, 2 kilometers south of Puerto del Rosario.

Lanzarote, Calle La Pesca 26; popular with the locals. **Benjamin**, Calle León y Castillo 137; Canary-French cuisine. *STREET CAFÉ:* **Tinguaro**, Plaza de España; perfect for watching the bustling crowds.

Casa Museo Unamuno, near the church, Calle Virgen del Rosario; Tue-Fri 10 am-1 pm & 5-8 pm, Sat and Sun 10:30 am-1 pm, closed Mon; admission free.

DISCOS: **Taifa**, Calle Juan Tadeo Cabrera 2. **La Fábrica**, in a factory on the road to Tetir.

Red Cross: Avda. de la Constitución 3, tel: 928 851 376. **Police**: Avda. de Juan Béthencourt, tel: 928 850 909.

POST OFFICE: Calle Primer de Mayo 58, tel: 928 850412.

TAXI: Tel: 928 850 059 and 928 850 216. *BUS:* Central bus stop at the corner of Avda. de la Constitución and Calle Léon y Cstilloy, operates hourly 7 am-2 pm and 4-8 pm; stops along the route include: the parish church of Nuestra Señora del Rosario, the market, Playa Blanca and the hospital.

Patronato de Turismo: Calle Primero de Mayo 33, tel: 928 530 844, fax: 928 851 695; Mon-Fri 8 am-3 pm.

THE NORTH

CORRALEJO

Hotel Riu Palace Tres Islas, Avda. de las Grandes Playas, tel: 928 535 700, fax: 928 535 858. Large complex near the dunes.

Hotel La Posada, Calle María Santana Figueroa 10, tel: 928 867 344, fax: 928 536 352. Pleasant, central, pool on the roof. **Hoplaco**, Avda. Generalisimo Franco, tel/fax: 928 866 040. Shady garden, simple, comfortable apartments. **Hotel Corralejo**, Calle Colón 12, tel: 928 535 246. Clean, central location, popular w/windsurfers and backpackers.

APARTMENTS: **Los Barqueros**, Avda. Grandes Playas, tel: 928 535 251, fax: 928 866 040; grounds with a palm garden, discounts for children.

Restaurante / Cantina Méxicana Pancho Villa, Calle Prim 16, tel: 928 535 014; Mexican, Tue-Thu 5 pm-midnight. **Sagar**, Calle Lepanto/Avda. Juan Carlos I, tel: 928 867 301; Indian and vegetarian, Tue-Thu 6-11:30 pm. **Vicoletto**, Calle La Ballena 6; close to the harbor, nice pizzeria, bar, closed Wed. **Don Juan** and **Café de París**, Avda. Generalisimo Franco; two good cafés, central location, they bake their own cakes.

The Big Blue, Avda. Grandes Playas 3, tel: 928 867 411. Blue stylish bar with a sea aquarium, live performances and parties. In the summer daily 6 pm-2:30 am, in the winter from 8 pm. Some largely British **surfer bars** in the Centro Atlántico, end of Avda. Generalisimo Franco, e.g., **Sandpiper** (English breakfast).

BOAT TRIPS: From Corralejo to the Isla de los Lobos and El Papagayo (Lanzarote) with **Catamaran Visión Submarina**, tel: 928 509 810/820. Or try the glass-bottomed boat **El Majorero**, info at the kiosk at the entrance to the pedestrian area; daily 9 am-noon and 6:30-9:30 pm.

DEEP-SEA FISHING: With the catamaran **Pez Velero,** from Corralejo, tel: 928 866 173; daily except Sun.

MOTORCYCLES / MOUNTAIN BIKES: **Mal Fun Club**, Avda. General Franco, tel: 928 867 541, 928 535 152; Mon-Sun 9 am-1 pm, Mon-Sat also 6-9 pm. Motorcycle, scooter, trike and mountain bike rentals. **Vulcano Biking**, Calle Acorazado España 10, tel: 928 535 706. Bicycle rentals, organized tours, special offers are also available for surfers.

DIVING: **Dive Center Corralejo**, tel: 928 866 243; Mon-Sat 8:30 am-1:30 pm. Boat trips with two dives.

TENNIS: Lessons at the **Academia Tenis Francisco González**, Avda. Islas Canarias 11, tel: 928 535 715, fax: 928 535 782.

SURFING / WINDSURFING: **Ineika Fun Center**, tel: 928 535 744. Surfing lessons, rentals. **Canary Surfing**, tel: 928 536 299. Windsurfing lessons, rentals. **Flag Beach Windsurf Center**, tel/fax: 928 535 539; **Ventura Surf**, tel/fax: 928 866 295. **Fanatic**, Avda. Grandes Playas, tel: 928 866 486, fax: 928 866 068.

HORSEBACK RIDING: Parque Holandés.

SPA: **Centro Mirak**, Parque Holandés, tel: 928 175 338.

Red Cross: Tel: 928 860 000. **Clinica Médica Brisamar**, Avda. Generalisimo Franco, tel: 928 536 402; open 24 hours. **International Medical Center**, Avda. Generalisimo Franco 13, in the Hotel Duna Park, tel: 928 536 432. The center's doctors also make house calls daily 9 am-8 pm.

POST OFFICE: Calle Lepanto 31, tel: 928 535 055.

SEA VOYAGES: **Naviera Armas**, office at the harbor, tel: 928 867 080. **Líneas Fred Olsen**, at the harbor, tel: 928 535 090. *TAXI:* Tel: 928 866 108.

The tourist mini-train **Mini-Tren** travels through town, from Avda. Generalisimo Franco to the dunes, every half hour; daily 9:30 am-11:30 pm.

i Oficina de Información y Turismo: Plaza Pública de Corralejo, tel: 928 866 235, fax: 928 866 186; Mon-Fri 9 am-2 pm and 4-7 pm. Information is also available in English.

EL COTILLO

Apartamentos Cotillo Lagos, Urbanización Los Lagos, tel: 928 175 388/389, fax: 928 852 099; near the beach.

Panadería/Pastelería **Los Cabezones**, Calle Santo Tomás, tel: 928 538 668, good bread. **Bar Restaurante La Marisma**, Calle Santo Tomás, tel: 928 538 543, good paella, seafood, fish. **Restaurante Azurro**, north of town, tel: 928 175 360; very fresh fish, pasta. **Ice Cream Parlor Heilo de Luna**, Calle Hermanas del Castillo 50, tel: 928 538 666; serves fruit juices, milkshakes and ice cream that is made on site.

DIVING: **El Cotillo Diving**, Coto Grande de Mascona 3, tel/fax: 928 175 011; lessons, rentals.

POST OFFICE: Calle Santo Domingo, tel: 928 538 539.

ISLA DE LOS LOBOS

Simple campground with no extra comforts located between El Puertito and Playa de la Calera. Otherwise camping is not allowed on the island.

LA OLIVA

Museo La Cilla (former tithe house); Tue-Sun 10:30 am-6:30 pm, closed Mon; **Centro de Arte Canario Casa Mané** (Canarian Art Center), tel: 928 868 233; daily 10 am-5 or 6 pm.

Caminata, Villaverde near La Oliva, tel: 928 535 010 (6-7 pm). Organized hiking tours.

Casa Marcos, in Villaverde, north of La Oliva, tel: 928 868 285; Fri-Wed 9:30 am-3 pm and 4-7 pm, closed Thu. Ceramics and Canarian handicrafts. **La Ermita**, ceramic workshop outside La Oliva; Mon-Sat 9 am-6 pm.

POST OFFICE: Calle Franco 14, tel: 928 868 065.

BUS: Route 7 from Puerto del Rosario & El Cotillo, 3 x daily; Route 8 from Corralejo & El Cotillo, 7 x daily.

LAJARES

Café Central, surfer hangout with live music.

La Casa del Artesano y del Calado, tel: 928 868 341; daily 9 am-7 pm. Handicraft shop with restaurant (La Caldera), sells goat's cheese. **Artesanía Lajares**, handicraft center in the middle of the village, best known for its embroidery.

THE MIDWEST

AGUAS VERDES

Club Aguas Verdes, tel: 928 878 350, fax: 928 878 360. Quiet, remote, sport and fitness facilities.

ANTIGUA

Molino de Antigua, north of the town center, tel: 928 851 400, with restaurant; daily 10 am-6 pm.

POST OFFICE: Calle Peña Brito 11, tel: 928 878 516.

TAXI: Tel: 928 878 011.

HANDICRAFT MARKET: Held on the second Sunday of the month; 10 am-6 pm.

BETANCURIA

Restaurante Casa Santa María, tel: 928 878 782. Renovated mansion, excellent and expensive. Lamb, smoked salmon, crafts, ceramics, agrarian products.

Mirador Morro Velosa, observation point, Canarian restaurant; daily 10 am-6 pm. **Iglesia/Museo de Arte Sacro**, Calle Alcalde Carmelo Silvera; Mon-Fri 9:30 am-5 pm, Sat 9:30 am-2 pm, closed Sun. **Museo Arqueológico**, Calle Roldán, tel: 928 878 241; Tue-Sat 10 am-5 pm, Sun 11 am-2 pm, closed Mon.

BUS: Route 2, from Puerto del Rosario, Mon-Fri 2 x daily. *TAXI:* Tel: 928 878 094.

LA PARED

Bar Restaurante El Camello, tel: 928 549 090/1; Tue-Sun 1 pm-midnight; Spanish regional dishes.

GOLF: **Driving Range**, tel/fax: 928 161 052/62; daily 10 am-6 pm. For professionals and beginners.

PÁJARA

Bar Restaurante La Fonda, in the town center, Calle Nuestra Señora de Regla 23, tel: 928 161 625; Tue, Wed and Thu 9:30 am-11 pm. Grill specialties.

TISCAMANITA

Centro de Interpretación de los Molinos, windmill museum, tel: 928 851 400; daily 10 am-6 pm.

VEGA RÍO PALMA

⊕ **Centro de Salud**, Calle San Sebastián, tel: 928 878 455.

THE SOUTH AND SOUTHEAST

LAS PLAYITAS

✖ **Casa Victor**, Calle Juan Soler 22, tel: 928 870 970; one of the island's best fish restaurants.

CALETA DE FUSTES

🛏 ⊗⊗ **Barceló Club Castillo**, east of the harbor, tel: 928 163 046, fax: 928 163 042. Pleasant, well-tended bungalow complex; tennis, squash, windsurfing, diving.

✖ **Bar Restaurante Puerto Castillo**, at the harbor, second floor, tel: 928 163 100/101; Tue-Sun 6-11 pm. Excellent international and vegetarian cooking.

🍸 *DISCO:* **La Polca**, Carretera General.

🤿 *DIVING:* **Dressel Divers Club International**, tel: 928 163 554. Diving lessons, free beginners' course. Similar offers from: **El Castillo**, on the break water, tel: 928 878 100. *WINDSURFING:* **Escuela de Windsurfing del Castillo**, tel: 928 163 100.

SUBMARINE: The **Nautilus** leaves from the harbor.

ℹ **Urbanización Caleta Dorada**, tel: 928 163 286; Mon-Fri 8 am-3 pm, closed Sat and Sun.

COFETE

📷 Festivities focused around *Apañada*, the rounding up of the area's wild goats. The dates change so it is advisable to check at the Oficina de Turismo (tourist information office) in Jandía Playa.

COSTA CALMA

🛏 ⊗⊗⊗ **Risco del Gato**, Polígono D2, tel: 928 547 175, fax: 928 547 030. Bungalow hotel with pool, sauna, tennis, golf and a gourmet restaurant.

⊗⊗ **Bungalows Bahía Calma**, tel: 928 547 158. Pretty bungalows on the beach.

🚕 *TAXI:* Tel: 928 547 032.

GRAN TARAJAL

🛏 ⊗ **Hostal Tamonante**, Calle Juan Carlos I, tel: 928 870 348 and 928 162 472. Small and clean; the only place to spend the night, popular with backpackers.

🍸 *DISCO:* **Roma**, Avda. Paco Hiero, near the beach.

⊕ **Centro de Salud**, Calle Tindaya 2, tel: 928 870 889.

📷 *POST OFFICE:* Plaza de la Candelaria, tel: 928 870 334.

🚕 *TAXI:* Tel: 928 870 059.

📷 **Fiesta Jurada de San Miguel**, Oct. 8-13. An extravagant history play that celebrates the victory of local farmers over a troop of invading English pirates in the Battle of Tamacite, in 1740.

JANDÍA PLAYA

🛏 ⊗⊗⊗ **Hotel Club Jandía Princess**, Urbanización Esquinzo, tel: 928 544 089, fax: 928 544 097. Andalusian-Moorish style, six pools, six tennis courts, 20-kilometer-long sandy beach. **Hotel Iberostar Palace**, Urbanización Las Gaviotas, tel: 928 540 444, fax: 928 540 405. Just outside town, long sandy beach, three pools, squash, sailing, windsurfing and diving.

✖ **Restaurante Don Carlos**, Edificio Don Carlos, at the Robinson Club, tel: 928 540 485; Spanish cuisine, large portions, closed Tue.

🤿 *ROBINSON CLUB:* Tennis & diving for guests of the **Robinson Club**; windsurfing courses & catamaran excursions open to non-guests, tel: 928 541 375/376. Similar offers at **Club Aldiana**, tel: 928 541 447/448.

DIVING: **Barakuda Club**, next to Residencia Atlántic on the main street, tel: 928 541 418, fax: 928 541 417.

WINDSURFING / MOUNTAIN BIKING: **Pro Center**, Hotel Sol Gorriones, tel: 928 547 025/026/050, fax: 928 870 850.

⊕ **Centro Médico**, tel: 928 540 420 and 928 541 543.

ℹ **Oficina de Turismo:** Avda. del Saladar, tel: 928 540 776, fax: 928 541 023.

LA LAJITA

🏛 **Zoo Parque Los Camellos**, tel: 928 161 135; daily 9 am-7:30 pm. Dromedary and pony rides.

MORRO JABLE

🛏 ⊗⊗⊗ **Hotel Riu Calypso**, Carretera General, tel: 928 541 522, fax: 928 540 730; on the beach.

⊗ **Hostal Maxorata**, Calle Maxorata 31, tel: 928 540 725 and 928 540 474; simple, popular with backpackers. **Pensión Omahy**, Calle Maxorata 6, tel: 928 541 254; for backpackers.

✖ **Restaurante La Gaviota**, on the beach promenade; fish, live Canarian music.

📷 *POST OFFICE:* Plaza Pública, tel: 928 540 373.

📷 *SEA VOYAGES:* **Naviera Armas**, tel: 928 542 113 and 928 542 457.

TAXI: Tel: 928 541 257.

ℹ **Oficina de Tourismo**, in the Centro Comercial, Avda. del Saladar, tel: 928 540 776.

TARRAJALEJO

🛏 ⊗⊗ **Hotel Tofio**, on the beach, tel: 928 161 001, fax: 928 161 028; pool, disco, sports facilities. Horseback riding in hotel's **Centro Hípico**, tel: 928 161 351.

📷 *BUS:* Route 1, from Puerto del Rosario and Morro Jable, 4-8 x daily.

Fuerteventura

THE WINDMILL ROUTE

Today it is windsurfers who, particularly during the summer, enjoy the wind and waves caused by the constantly blowing northeasterly trade winds. In the past it was the island's millers who availed themselves of the wind's power.

Fuerteventura has been the granary of the Canarian archipelago since the early 16th century. Initially the harvested wheat had to be ground by hand because the first windmills didn't appear until about a hundred years later.

Once they did arrive, they were modeled on the ones in Castille on the Spanish mainland, with circular, slightly conical 10- to 15-meter-high towers and a conical wooden roof that, along with the sails, could be turned to take advantage of the wind regardless of the direction it was

Previous Pages: A windsurfer's paradise – here on the Playa de Corralejo. Above and Right: A crushing mill and a "male" windmill in Centro de Artesania Molino in Antigua.

blowing. The mill was driven by four to six canvas-covered sails. Whenever it was not in use, the *molino macho* ("male" mill) was stripped of its sails, which were covered with wax to increase the resistance they offered the wind.

The thinner "female" mill, or *molina*, was developed by a miller from the nearby island of La Palma during the early 19th century. Although they are less complex than their "male" counterparts, they are more efficient at grinding smaller quantities. A typical *molina* consists of a wooden tower to which the sails are affixed. The wind power is transferred to the grinding stone via a connecting rod. With the help of a wooden pole the entire construction can be turned into the wind.

In the meantime, wheat cultivation has been given up in favor of the cultivation of tomatoes. In total there are 38 disused mills on the island, 15 of which are *molina*s. Unfortunately, many of the mills are in ruins, although government plans to subsidize their restoration are in the works.

Most of them are located in the island's interior, since this is where the corn, which was used to make *gofio*, a local specialty, was usually grown.

Some years ago Fuerteventura's governmental tourist office established a "Windmill Route" that leads past 13 well-preserved mills and is certainly worth a day trip. They are not particularly well signed, but since these splendid showpieces were built on hilltops, they can easily be seen from afar.

The *Ruta de los Molinos* begins in the north, in the center of **Corralejo**, with two somewhat decayed mills (*molina* and *molino*). From here you can head in a southerly direction (toward La Oliva), turning west after ten kilometers. Ten kilometers further on you can see two more *molino* in **El Roque**. (On the way you can pass through **Lajares**, with a charming ensemble consisting of a chapel and a pair of windmills in its **Casas de Arriba** quarter.) Back on the main road, just before **La Oliva**, you can see two more *molino*s in **Villaverde**.

In the central mountains you can see a six-armed *molino* in **Tefía** as well as the two windmills in **Llanos de la Concepción**.

A functioning "male" mill can be seen at the **Centro de Artesania Molino** in **Antigua**. You can also take a look inside the mill every day between 10:00 a.m. and 6:00 p.m. In addition to the windmill there is a cactus garden, art exhibits with paintings by local artists, a handicrafts store and a small café.

Near the northern village of **Tiscamanita** another functioning *molino* can be seen at the **Centro de Interpretación de los Molinos**. In the adjacent building, the former residence of the miller's family, grinding wheels and equipment can be viewed every day between 10:00 a.m. and 6:00 p.m. On your way to Tiscamanita you pass two *molino*s in **Valles de Ortega**.

Save Fuerteventura's most beautiful *molina* for your return journey. It is located in **Puerto de Lajas**, five kilometers north of **Puerto del Rosario**.

FUERTEVENTURA UP CLOSE

As early as the drive from the airport to their hotels visitors to Fuerteventura will be charmed by the island's fascinating lunar-like landscape and the variety of its muted earth tones and pastels. Endless plains that are covered with lava stones and the cones of ancient volcanoes that have been flattened by centuries of wind and rain contrast with wide-open sandy spaces along the coast that are edged by cliffs against which the surf constantly pounds. After just one look at Fuerteventura many visitors decide that they won't be satisfied just looking at it through the windows of a bus or car. They need to get out and experience its beauty and wonders up close.

After the first standard excursions to the dunes of Corralejo on the north coast, and the Punta Pesebre in the south, some visitors may feel inspired to tackle a somewhat longer walking tour, perhaps something a little bit further off the beaten track. Fuerteventura, however, is not the kind of place where you can take an easy walk for a couple of hours. Before heading out for a day of serious hiking you will need to make sure you have sturdy hiking boots that support your ankles, serious sun protection for your head and skin, a backpack with some food and, above all, plenty of drinking water.

Hiking on Isla de los Lobos

Isla de los Lobos, which you can easily explore in one day, is most accessible from Fuerteventura's northern coast. Visitors coming from further south have to allow for an additional two-hour trip just to get to the departure point.

Several small boats to the tiny neighboring island leave from the **harbor of Corralejo** every day about 10:00 a.m. Tickets can be purchased at booths in the harbor and the pedestrian zone.

Above: The boat crossing from Corralejo to Isla de los Lobos. Right: Easily mastered – the descent from the volcano Montaña de Lobos.

The crossing only takes about 20 minutes and ends at a small dock. From here a hiking path leads into the interior. After only a few hundred meters you will have to decide whether you want to circumnavigate the island clockwise or counterclockwise. If you go to the left, you will first ascend the 127-meter-high Montaña de Lobos, followed by a hike to the lighthouse and a stop at El Puertito for a well-deserved drink. If you choose this route you should allow for three to four hours of walking after you reach the top of the mountain.

After a ten-minute walk on the well-paved path you will reach **Playa de la Calera**, a beautifully located sandy bay. From here you can get a good look at your first destination, the **Montaña de Lobos**, in the distance. A steep, switchback trail leads up a rocky slope – since there is no shade this demands considerable physical effort – but after 20 minutes the climb is over. Once you have reached at the top you will be rewarded with a fantastic view of the entire island. The dunes of

Corralejo can be seen in the distance, separated from the island by the strait of **El Río**, which is just a river that is a mere two-kilometers wide. In a northeasterly direction, on the other hand, the south coast of Lanzarote comes into view.

The mountain's rugged peak is an ideal breeding ground for the herring gull. This silver-colored seabird with its yellow beak is mostly seen in flocks. Ospreys, however, are only be seen singly, and then only if you are very, very lucky.

The next stage is the automatic **lighthouse** of **Faro de Lobos** in the far northeast of the island. On your way there, you will see so-called *hornitos* (little ovens) to the right and left of the path. These mounds, sometimes small, sometimes bigger, that emerged as gas bubbles escaped from the lava and are named after their typical shape. The shade of the lighthouse is a good place to take a break and enjoy the view of Lanzarote.

In the northern part of the island there are several large salty meadows that are periodically flooded by seawater. Because of the salt content of the water a specific type of vegetation has established itself here and numerous migrating birds flock to this region in search of food.

The way back to the dock follows the east coast in a southerly direction, past a former Agave plantation. Plenty of these plants, the fibers of which were once used in the manufacturing of rope for ships, can now be seen growing wild all over the area.

Just when you really feel like having a drink, the few houses of **El Puertito** seem to appear in the middle of nowhere. Since many of the restaurants are now open throughout the day, there is a sufficient selection of food and beverages. If you have enough time left before having to catch your return ride, you can take a refreshing dip in the sea at the local bay, which is protected from the strong surf by a couple of distant cliffs. Since the dock is no more than a few minutes walk from El Puertito, you can relax and take your time before you return.

Ascent to Pico de la Zarza

If you are spending your holiday further south in Costa Calma, Jandía Playa or Morro Jable you will probably prefer to explore that part of the island first. A good "warm-up hike" is on the Jandía Peninsula at **Punta Pesebre**, where you can comfortably walk in either direction along the rocky coast with its roaring surf.

Eventually you might be seized with the desire to climb the **Pico de la Zarza** (also called **Jandía**) – at 807 meters above sea level certainly the highest peak on Fuerteventura. Even if the ascent does

Right: Constantly crossing your path – the funny little North African chipmunk, a member of the rodent family, was brought to Fuerteventura in 1965. Today these prolific breeders can be seen across the island.

not lead through terrain of exhilarating beauty, the view from the summit will exceed your expectations. To the west you can see Playa de Barlovento and Playa de Cofete, ending at Punta Pesebre. To the south Playa de Sotavento stretches out below. Right at the foot of the mountain you can distinctly make out Villa Winter as well as the houses of Cofete. To the northeast the foothills of Jandía's massif merge into the dunes of La Pared. Just beyond the dunes you can see where the mountains around Betancuria begin. On a clear day you can take in the entire east coast right up to the lighthouse in El Cotillo. And, if you are very, very lucky, you might even be able to spot the outline of the neighboring island of Gran Canaria.

Start your ascent of Pico de la Zarza in **Jandía Playa** at the Hotel Riu Ventura. The path leads to the east for a short while before heading up a mountain ridge, with an elevation gain of about 200 meters. After a gentle uphill section the real climb starts. The path is well signed and easily recognizable, particularly since your destination is always in good view. Allow for about four hours of walking for the round-trip. It is essential to wear good hiking boots and good sun protection, and you should bring plenty of drinking water and some easily digestible food. You will probably want to bring a camera along as well, since people, e.g., you, standing on the summit in front of the breathtaking background makes a beautiful souvenir photo.

Roaming on the Cliffs of Playa de los Muertos

Another interesting hike that you can enjoy equally well from the vacation centers in the south or from those situated in the north, begins in the mid-west near **Ajuy** at **Playa de los Muertos**, the "beach of the dead." This dramatic-sounding name is a relic from the time

when Jean Béthancourt tried to conquer the island from the western side. He did not succeed, however, owing to the fierce resistance of the island's native population. Since a number of Guanches fell in the battles, the beach came to be known as Playa de los Muertos.

At the northern end of the bay, which is filled with black sand, a small hiking path begins, winding its way upwards through the limestone rocks. Once you reach the top of the cliffs (ca. 100 meters high) an amazing view of the beach, surrounded by thundering waves, stretches out below. The path, safeguarded by wooden railings, follows the rocky ledge for about one kilometer before reaching a observation platform. From there a rocky flight of steps snakes steeply downwards to the mouths of two giant natural caves. The strong breakers thundering incessantly against the offshore rocks make a deafening noise, but both caves may be explored without any problems or extra flashlights since sufficient light comes in through the entrances.

Once you are back on the observation platform, follow the path, which runs parallel to the cliffs and directly above the caves, in a northerly direction. A short distance later you will reach a spot where about ten iron tubes, each with a diameter of half a meter, break through the ceiling of the rearmost cave, which lies just below. In earlier times limestone was mined up here on the rock plateau, and was transported through the tubes, down to the bay where it was then loaded onto waiting ships.

After another two kilometers the worn path leads into the **Barranco de la Peña**. The 20-meter-high natural archway **Arco del Jurado** is at its far end. The foam from the incoming breakers splashes surprisingly high onto the nearby rocks. As you can imagine, this is not safe to swim, however, you could spend hours on end watching the powerful play of the waves. After returning along the same route, you should try one of the delicious fish dishes that are served at the small **beach restaurant** at Playa de los Muertos in Ajuy.

53

EXPLORING THE ISLAND
BY BICYCLE

Fuerteventura is the second-largest island of the Canarian archipelago, after Tenerife. Because of the its long, narrow shape places Corralejo in the north and Morro Jable in the south are nearly 100 kilometers apart. At first this distance might give the impression that the island is only suitable for serious cyclists, however, if you choose the right routes and distances anyone that can ride a bike can explore Fuerteventura's fascinating landscape on two wheels. And, besides getting a little exercise, you will experience the island in a way that is just not possible from a bus or car.

You can start with shorter day trips on a rented bicycle, from Morro Jable to Playa de Cofete, or from Corralejo to El Cotillo for example. On these rides you will

Above and Right: Riding up the Morro de la Cruz and the view from the top ... of the beautiful Betancuria Valley.

quickly realize what it is that matters most when cycling on Fuerteventura: sunscreen and water! Make sure to take sufficient sun protection for your head and arms and carry plenty of drinking water, since bars and restaurants along the way are rare. You should also keep two other important points in mind. One, off-road cycling on a mountain bike with full-suspension is much more pleasant than on one without. And two, any tours in a northeasterly direction can be made more difficult by strong winds.

If you follow these basic rules, are in reasonably good physical condition and have a sturdy mountain bike you might even consider covering a major part of the island this way.

A Tour of the Interior

This tour, including all of the stages, is about 140 kilometers long. It leads in a circular route around the island and may be started from a number of different points. If you are staying in Corralejo in the north, for instance, take the road to Betancuria, via La Oliva and Tefía. If you are staying in the south, Morro Jable perhaps, follow the main road to Matas Blancas. You might even be lucky enough to get help from a friendly bus driver who will give you a lift on this dull part of the journey, which has plenty of traffic.

Our description of this tour begins in Puerto del Rosario, where ships from the neighbouring islands put ashore.

From **Puerto del Rosario** ride the gradual uphill to **Casillas del Ángel** and from there continue on to **Llanos de la Concepción**, where you can already see the mountains in the distance. From here the route leads past the palm oasis of **Valle de Santa Inés** and up the **Morro de la Cruz** (676 meters), which affords a wonderful view of **Betancuria**. After recovering from the climb you can easily coast down into the village, which is a suitable place to stop for a little break.

An attractive stage begins as you leave Betancuria, where the road leads past **Vega de Río de las Palmas** with its countless palms. The next pass begins a short distance further, before the road leads down again and into **Pájara** where a number of charming restaurants invite you to linger.

(If you plan to return to Puerto del Rosario on the same day, you might want take the connecting road from Pájara, via Toto, to Tuineje and return from there via Antigua. This detour pretty much cuts the tour in half.)

Otherwise you can continue cycling from Pájara towards **La Pared**. Despite the sweat-inducing ascent that follows, your efforts will be fully rewarded by the fascinating mountain landscape and refreshing descent.

From La Pared the route covers the narrowest part of Fuerteventura, leading through a most impressive landscape of dunes and over to **Matas Blancas**, which is located on the southeastern side of the island.

From Matas Blancas you ride to **Tarajalejo**, then on to the **Tesejerague / La Florida** turn-off. This stage is about 15 kilometers long and the road is, unfortunately, quite busy.

After you reach the turn-off a quiet side road leads through the barren region that is known as the *malpais*, the "badlands." Follow this road up to **Tuineje**.

From Tuineje onwards the route once again becomes more varied. You will ride past palms, cacti and ruined windmills to **Antigua**. Just before you reach the church turn to the right onto a side road that leads to **Triquivijate**. Then, after another short climb, you can coast down into Puerto del Rosario.

Kilometer Indications: Puerto del Rosario – Casillas del Ángel 12 km, Casillas del Ángel – Betancuria 17 km, Betancuria – Pájara 16 km, Pájara – La Pared 27 km, La Pared – Matas Blancas 6 km, Matas Blancas – Tarajalejo 10 km, Tarajalejo – Tuineje 18 km, Tuineje – Antigua 12 km, Antigua – Puerto del Rosario 21 km; 139 km total.

THE CHILD-FRIENDLY ISLAND

Fuerteventura's near-perfect climate makes this island an attractive year-round vacation destination for singles and families alike. The few beaches that are well protected from the wind are generally dotted with countless children playing with their little buckets and shovels, having a blast in this never-ending sandbox. The water that laps the edge of the beach is usually so shallow that parents can happily watch their offspring from a relaxing distance while sunbathing in their deck chairs.

Another benefit that should make a vacation to Fuerteventura more enjoyable for parents is the wide variety of "children's entertainment" that is on offer. Today every hotel and club resort offers some kind of baby-sitting service, but the quality of care can vary greatly. Some hotels simply put a few toys in a tiny room, and assign a Spanish-speaking person to simply hang around and keep an eye on things during opening hours. Other hotels fill their playrooms with all manner of toys, games and arts and crafts projects, and provide several bilingual young adults to supervise the children and activities. Some resorts even offer a varied program of beach attractions, excursions, children's discos and other kid-friendly activities. Of course, such attractive children's programs will affect the price of your vacation.

Clubs Suitable for Children

In the south we recommend the **Stella Canaris Holiday Park**. In the middle of this area there is a giant children's amusement park with a Mini-Club. Furthermore, a varied entertainment program is on offer, with theater productions, fash-

Right: A great place for kids to have fun without their parents – on the playground at the Barceló Club El Castillo.

ion shows, pirate parties, painting competitions, horseback riding and a day at the beach.

The grounds of the Stella Canaris include a bird sanctuary that is also open to non-residents. During a stroll through the attractively designed, palm-filled complex you can observe several exotic species of the bird kingdom. There is also a pool, which is where most children prefer to do their swimming.

Caleta de Fustes offers the best beach conditions for vacationers. The seabed of the incredibly wide sandy beach slopes gently and the beach is protected from the waves by an offshore harbor jetty. The water, which is just knee-deep in many places, is an ideal place to learn how to swim or windsurf. Just behind the beach is the **Barceló Club El Castillo**, a spacious complex with 382 apartments in terraced houses and free-standing bungalows. Each unit has a terrace, balcony, a fully equipped kitchenette, a living and dining room, a bedroom, a television set and a telephone. Just in case your children get tired of visiting the beach, there are two nice pools for them, as well as a playground and a Mini-Club.

The ultimate in children's care, however, is the **Robinson Club** at the Esquinzo Playa. In the "Roby Club" there is a nursery for babies and for children aged three to six there is a full-time children's activity and care program; in the peak tourist season it is extended to include children of all ages. Numerous members of the staff organize treasure hunts, beach games as well as painting and handicraft classes. The swimming lessons offer range covering everything from baby swimming to obtaining the "Little Sea Horse" certificate. Additional highlights include a wading pool, a multipurpose sports field, an adventure pool, table tennis, and a children's movie theater and a disco for the evenings. It isn't just the kids that get the royal treatment, however. Parents are also well cared-for

at this holiday resort. All kinds of sporting activities such as surfing, tennis and beach volleyball are always available. Last but not least, if you still get bored, the internet café with its many computers awaits you with an alternative form of entertainment. Of course, the prices at this top-of-the-range vacation resort are rather high, so you will want to make sure that you are ready to take advantage of its round-the-clock entertainment opportunities.

Keeping The Kids Amused

Once you have settled the question of where to stay, it is time to go on some excursions with your kids.

A double attraction awaits you near the fishing village of La Lajita. The **Zoo Parque de los Camellos** is both a **zoo** and a **dromedary station**. Inside the zoo you can watch the monkeys, crocodiles and peacocks, the highlight for many children being the **parrot show** that takes place several times a day.

Across the street from the zoo the dromedaries await their riders. Their peculiar saddles offer one place on each side of the hump. In the interest of the animals, two persons of similar weight are always transported at the same time. If necessary, stones are used as ballast to provide the required balance. Smaller children, however, may be seated in the middle between two adults. On the command of the *camellero* the dromedaries stand up one after the other and the caravan sets in motion. With a lot of rocking and rolling you are taken on a leisurely excursion through the countryside, accompanied by the wisecracks of the camel driver. Once a day the dromedary ride leads to the nearby bay and while passengers eat their picnic and swim in the sea, the dromedaries take a well-earned break and relax in the sand.

At least once during their visit the children that are staying at the Barceló Club in Caleta de Fustes urge their parents to take them to the nearby **Hipo-Park**. A bouncy castle and numerous other attrac-

tions provide a splendid alternative to the beach, which means the Hipo-Park can at times be rather crowded.

Go-carting is not just available to adult fans of motor sports. Children that are seven and older may also test their abilities on the go-cart course near Ocios del Sur. There are safety helmets for everybody and parents may either race against each other and their children or relax and enjoy a café con leche while watching the terrace.

The wind blows constantly on Fuerteventura, which makes it ideal for **kite flying**. This activity, which is normally only available in the spring, works beautifully on local beaches all year round. The German Michael Steinemer has specialized in kite flying and every day he visits a different beach with his colorful and fantastic models. Without having to spend a lot of time and money, non-experts can buy a simple steerable kite and fly it right away. Near the small village of Valles de Ortega Michael Steinemer has established a workshop where he designs and makes his own kites. He also offers workshops to those who are interested in learning how to make their own kites.

If your children enjoy sea adventures, they will love what is waiting for them in the harbor of Morro Jable. On the **pirate ship Pedra Sartaña** the sails are set at 10:00 a.m. and, after hoisting the pirate flag, off they sail to the open sea! As soon as all the children have dressed-up and put on their pirate make up, the games can start. After their great adventure they are given a snack and can take a refreshing swim in the ocean.

Above: Great fun for children and adults alike – the dromedary caravan in La Lajita. Right: Tired but safely returned from their adventures at sea – little "pirates" back on land in Morro Jable.

Unremitting Holiday Pleasure

It is always wise to take the same precautions during any outdoor activity as you would when sunbathing, so don't for-

get to bring a hat and plenty of sunscreen, which is a must not only for children, but for adults as well. Particularly during the winter months, when your skin doesn't usually have much of a tan, sunscreen should have be at least PF 25. In order to avoid getting burned, children should always wear a hat with a brim and a loose, long-sleeved shirt while they play on the beach. And why not adopt the sensible Spanish custom of taking a relaxing siesta in your hotel room during the early afternoon, when the sun burns the strongest?

In case one of your children gets hurt or sick, you can contact an English-speaking doctor in any of the tourist resorts. In the big hotels and club resorts there is usually doctor with office hours every day, or receptionist at your hotel will certainly know the phone number or address of the nearest hospital or medical clinic. (See page 89 for more information about medical emergencies and pharmacies.)

Purchasing the basic necessities for small children is no problem whatsoever on Fuerteventura. In every drugstore and supermarket you will be able to find a wide selection of baby food, diapers and whatever else you may need.

Addresses:

Stella Canaris Holiday Park, Av. del Salada, Jandía Playa, tel: 928 873 399.

Barceló Club El Castillo, Caleta del Fuste, tel: 928 163 100.

Robinson Club, Jandía Playa, tel: 928 541 375.

All three resorts can be booked through your travel agent.

Zoo Park de los Camellos, La Lajita, located on the road between Morro Jable and Tarajalejo, daily 9 am to 7 pm.

Hipo-Park, Caleta de Fustes, daily 10 am to 10 pm.

Gran Karting (go-carts), Ocios del Sur, daily 10 am to 6 pm.

Cometas Fuerteventura, Michael Steinemer, Valles de Ortega (just south of town and to the right), tel: 928 174 618 or in Germany +(49) 171 463 9972.

Pirate Ship Pedra Sartaña, in the harbor of Morro Jable, tel: 670 745 191.

PLANTS AS SURVIVAL SPECIALISTS

Just about every plant aficionado has at least one cactus on his windowsill. This popularity cacti stems largely from the fact that in many countries cacti don't naturally occur. Furthermore, the prickly plants are relatively easy to care for; since they hardly ever need to be watered they are almost impossible to kill.

On Fuerteventura, an island with relatively little precipitation, the only plants that have a real chance to survive in the wild are those that can tolerate lengthy dry seasons. According to historical travelers' accounts, during the 19th century Fuerteventura was wooded and quite humid, but today its semi-desert climate is an ideal habitat for a variety of thick-leaved, waxy succulents. However, even

Above: The Candelabra euphorbia is often mistaken for a cactus because of its spines and cactus-like shape. Right: The fruit of the fig cactus (Opuntie) is sweet and tasty.

they cannot exist entirely without water, which on Fuerteventura truly is a rare commodity. Rain seldom falls from the sky, the clouds of the trade winds don't often leave dewdrops on leaves, and what little water there is quickly evaporates in the intense sunlight. As a result, optimal storage of this indispensable commodity is necessary for survival, a principle that succulents have mastered in a surprising variety of ways.

Even an amateur should immediately notice that most plants in arid regions have a large number of thorns or spines, with the cactus itself being the best-known example. These spines perform the function of leaves, providing the plant with a constant supply of moisture. Other plants, like the relatively rare **Hawthorn's aeonium** (*Aeonium haworthii*, commonly known as pinwheels), a knee-high yellow Compositae that grows at altitudes above 400 meters, form fine hairs on the surface of their leaves. These hairs have water-storage properties and, since they reflect the sun like a mirror, they also protect the plants from drying out.

Other shrubs rely on the strength of their roots, which allow them to dig deep into the ground. With their amazingly long subterranean network of roots they are able to tap veins of ground water, or at least penetrate levels that retain a bit more moisture. A typical representative of this species of shrub is the yellow-blossomed **camel thorn** (*Acacia giraffae* or *Alhagi pseud-alhagi*) whose branches are highly flammable.

Some shrubs have yet another "trick" in store. They just "don hats" by extending their branches radially, from a single stem. It is wolf's-milk, or spurge, the most common plant on Fuerteventura, that is a perfect example of this adaptation. These Euphorbia account for the majority of all succulents. Fuerteventura's the most common species, King Juba wolf's-milk, also known as **taibaba**, is considered to be particularly fond of

salty areas and tends to grow along the island's coast and on Isla de los Lobos. Amazingly, it grows on stony ground and even on lava.

One plant that is often confused with a cactus is the **Candelabra euphorbia** or **Candelabra wolf's-milk** (Spanish *cardón*), which has columns that tower up to two meters into the sky. This plant may store water in its particularly thick-skinned stem. It prefers to grow on steep mountain cliffs and may live to be up to 100 years old. While the Candelabra wolf's-milk is endemic throughout the Canary Islands, the Jandía wolf's-milk, as indicated by its name, can only be found on Fuerteventura's Jandía Peninsula.

All Euphorbias, except for the Balsam wolf's-milk (*Euphorbia resinifera*), produce a slightly poisonous, milky liquid that prevents even the island's voracious wild goats from nibbling off their branches. This also comes in useful for other plants that are able to grow among the Euphorbias without falling victim to the voracious goats. Humans are the most likely to come into contact with the milk of the taibaba, whose twigs are particularly brittle. Children in particular should be told to make sure they don't to rub the sticky substance into their eyes or put their fingers into their mouths after touching a plant; it might lead to mild irritation of the mucous membranes. The numbing effect of this sap was already known to the Guanches, who successfully used it for fishing.

If, despite all of its sophisticated protection mechanisms, a succulent threatens to die due to a lack of water or illness, it will attempt to ensure the survival of its species. This is why most succulents bear countless blossoms just before perishing, the seeds of which will disperse in the immediate surroundings, safeguarding the survival of the next generation.

If you want to take some succulents home, you can buy small potted plants in special stores – there are even a few shops at the airport so you can grab one on the way to the plane!

STAYING IN THE COUNTRYSIDE

A couple was happy to snatch a last-minute vacation bargan. They were headed to Fuerteventura for just $400 per person, including flight, transfer, accommodation and half-board in a 3-star-hotel. However, they weren't happy for long. Through their room's thin walls they could hear the constantly blaring TV next door, the busy road right out their window made it impossible to fall asleep, and once fianlly got to sleep the night owls across the hall returned from a round of bar hopping just in time to wake them from their dreams. To top it all off, the food they were served reminded them of eating lunch in the school cafeteria.

Change of scene: In the glow of the setting sun four friends are on the patio of a free-standing finca, starting a fire in the fireplace. Later, when the sky is lit by coutless twinkling stars, they are sitting in front of the fire, drinking wine and enjoying the organic goat cheese the owner of the finca brought by. During the night not a single sound – apart from the chirping of crickets – disturbs their sleep.

Turismo Rural – gentle rural tourism in the countryside – is the motto according to which numerous visitors to the neighboring islands of Gran Canaria and Tenerife already spend their vacations, away from the tourist resorts and in the attractive countryside. And it isn't only tourists that are profiting. Inland regions acquire a new attractiveness, the decay of historical buildings is halted and locals make some extra money by selling their agricultural products to tourists. On Fuerteventura, however, this kind of tourism is still in its infancy.

Above: The finca El Sitio de Jaifa – authentically reconstructed from natural stones. Right: Even the bathroom decor is in harmony with the rustic setting and ambiance.

The Casa Rural El Sitio de Jaifa

One of the forerunners in the growing trend of spending one's vacation in rural,

but first-class surroundings was 40-year-old teacher named Norberto. A few years ago he bought a 200-year-old run-down farm building and the two hectares of land surrounding it. With tiresome work the foundation walls were rebuilt using natural stone, then the flat roof was reconstructed using reeds and mud.

Inside Norberto has covered the floor with earth-tone tiles and painted the walls in warm earthy colors. All of the furniture is made of solid pine. He has also spent countless hours doing all of the interior renovations. Now the various rooms are tastefully adorned with traditional inlayed stones and modern tiles. In addition to his consistent use of stones, Norberto has made sure that the finca's energy supply meets high environmentally-friendly standards. Solar panels and cells supply both the finca's electricity and its hot water.

There is more than enough space in the finca's four rooms (two double, two single) for six adults and a couple of children to sleep comfortably.

The only requests Norberto makes of his guests is that they economize their usage of electricity and water, treating both like the valuable resources they are, and that they treat the valuable and artistic furnishings with care. In turn they may enjoy the pleasure of staying at one of the most beautiful and comfortable fincas on the Canary Islands.

Apart from the finca's fully-equipped kitchen, there is a washing machine, a TV and stereo equipment. The real highlight of it all, however, is the bathroom, which could easily have come from a designer magazine.

The fince with the fine-sounding name of **Casa Rural El Sitio de Jaifa** is located about five kilometers west of Puerto del Rosario in completely quiet surroundings. The entire finca runs about 12,000 Ptas a day, which is very reasonable, especially if a number of people split the cost. Because of is relative isolation, a rental car is recommended – there is just one restaurant within easy reach. (Tel/fax: 928 861 124).

**SURFING THE WAVES
IN STRONG WINDS**

Although no one is sure of the origins of the name Fuerteventura, it has but one meaning for windsurfers: *fuerte viento* – the strong wind. The winds here measure between four and five on the Beaufort scale pretty much year round, and during the summer months the winds regularly measure six to eight the Beaufort scale. It is no wonder then that this is the number one vacation destination among European windsurfers. Once a year even the world elite meets here to compete in a World Cup competition at Playa de Sotavento. Fuerteventura isn't just for pros, however, most of the island's windsurfing schools also cater to beginners, offering classes in bays that are protected from strong winds and big waves.

Above: A windsurfer in his element. Right: Every imaginable variety of water sport is on offer to guests visiting Caleta de Fustes (Playa del Castillo).

Surfing enthusiasts, once they have decided to go to Fuerteventura, will have to decide if they want to take their own equipment or rent everything once they get there. If you decide to pay the extra $50 and take your board, appropriately protected of course, on the plane, you will have to deal with the difficulties of getting it from it from the airport to your hotel. If you plan to rent a car, be prepared to request, and pay for, a suitable roof rack when you make your reservation. Transportation in a charter bus might also be possible, assuming there aren't too many other boards that need to be transported. If you want to avoid all of these difficulties you can also rent everything once you get there. Local surfing centers rent excellent boards for around $100. You can even make reservations before you arrive.

Once you catch sight of all the wind-filled sails you will quickly come down with a bad case of "surf fever." However, the conditions on Fuerteventura take some getting used to, so be cautious and take it slowly at the beginning. People wanting to compare their skills with those of the experts, should at least have some experience with strong winds and have mastered the water start. It is better to invest a few hours practicing in calmer waters than literally getting out of your depth and exhausting yourself. Regardless of your skill level, you should ask about the current undertow conditions at one of the surf shops and, even during the summer, it is recommended that you wear a lightweight neoprene suit.

Where to Windsurf

Playa Barca, about five kilometers south of Costa Calma, is a windsurfing hotspot that, because of its location, is of particular interest to vacationers in the Morro Jable region. The journey there is best made on the main route and via the short connecting road to the Hotel Los Gorrines, where you will also find the

Surfing the Waves in Strong Winds

well-known Pro Center that belongs to René Egli, who is originally from Switzerland. An offshore sandbank forms a calm 500-meter-wide lagoon – a good place for beginners to practice. Beyond the sandbank experts amuse themselves in winds that, during the summer, measure up to nine on the Beaufort scale. High-speed races and the annual World Cup competition are regular events.

Another fascinating place to windsurf is **Flag Beach**, located in the north of the island, some five kilometer outside Corralejo, but before the two hotels in the dunes. There is a surfing center here, as well as a special feature particular to this region: several underwater reefs form rather high waves throughout the year. Just as at Playa Barca, the winds here blow mainly offshore. Lifeboats patrol both beaches and rescue those who are too exhausted to return to the beach on their own.

Surfers along the north coast, on the other hand, have to fend for themselves. The various local spots are considered to be a challenge for both man and material: there is a gusty wind, strong surf, unpredictable undertows, sharp-edged lava rocks and disagreeable sea urchins. Moreover, the journey to get here has to be made on a washboard dirt road. If you plan to surf here, you will certainly get the ultimate kick, however, be aware of the risks! If you get hurt there aren't any doctors nearby, and if you drift off there isn't a lifeboat to rescue you.

More relaxed surfing awaits you, however, at the beach in **Caleta de Fustes**. The harbor jetty keeps away wind and waves, and in the knee-deep water it is safe for even the youngest to practice, provided they are strong enough to pull the sail out of the water.

Addresses:

Pro Center – Playa Barca, Hotel Los Gorrines, tel: 928 547 425, fax: 928 547 000. Windsurf Center – Flag Beach, Corralejo, tel/fax: 928 535 539. Fanatic Fun Center – Caleta de Fustes, Avenida Grandes Playa, tel: 928 535 999, fax: 928 535 998.

FUERTEVENTURA'S MOST BEAUTIFUL BEACHES

Of all of the Canary Islands, Fuerteventura may boast of having, by far, the most beaches. *Vamos a la playa*, let's go to the beach – this is the true center of any vacation on Fuerteventura.

Playa de Sotavento

Over 20 kilometers of golden sandy beach, up to a few hundred meters wide in places, are located south of the holiday resorts of Costa Calma, on the southeastern coast of the Jandía Peninsula. As the name Sotavento suggests, the wind nearly always blows across the land out towards the sea. The direction of the wind, as well as some offshore sandbanks, keep big breakers away from the beach making it is safe for even children to swim here. The bad news, however, is that there is hardly any shade and almost no facilities, except at Playa Barca, a four-kilometer-long stretch of Playa de Sotavento. Here you can find several restaurants, such as Villa Esmeralda or the Hotel Los Gorrines. This region is a Mecca for windsurfers since it provides ideal conditions nearly all year round. At low tide extensive mud flats that are very inviting for walkers are exposed offshore.

Playa del Matorral

The seemingly endless string of private hotel beaches in the south begin at Morro Jable and stretch to a salty meadow north of the lighthouse on Jandía Playa. In the vicinity of the big hotels you may rent deck chairs and sunshades, and there are numerous kiosks, ice cream parlors and street cafés on the road that runs parallel

Right: Enjoy yourself at one of the tourists' favorite spots – the cafés and bars along the promenade in Morro Jable (Playa del Matorral).

to the beach. If you prefer somewhat quieter locations, however, just wander in a northerly direction from the lighthouse. Morro Jable's beach bars are very popular.

Playa de Juan Gómez

A beautiful and almost deserted sandy beach on the south coast, located some 15 kilometers from Morro Jable. It is only accessible from the unpaved road from Morro Jable towards Cofete and Punta Pesebre. Just before the exit to Cofete a trail forks off to the left, and leads down to the beach. The journey, however, can only be made with an off-road vehicle or on a mountain bike, and once you get to the beach there are no facilities.

Playa de Ojos

The "donkey beach" is located at the far end of the Jandía Peninsula, half-way between the few houses of Puerto de la Cruz and the lighthouse in Punta Pesebre. The tiny beach below the steeply sloping cliffs is only accessible via the unpaved road from Morro Jable, as is also is the case for the Playa de Juan Gómez. There are several restaurants in nearby Puerto de la Cruz and their fish (fresh) dishes are particularly good.

Playa de Cofete

This lonely and practically deserted sandy beach stretches for nearly 15 kilometers along the northern coast of the Jandía Peninsula. From here you can enjoy a marvelous view of the tiny hamlet of Cofete, and the Villa Winter, located on the mountainside and Pico de la Zarza, Fuerteventura's highest mountain peak. This beach is ideal for long walks, but there is no shade and the strong undertow makes swimming a dangerous enterprise. Very little is on offer apart from the small bar in Cofete and the dusty road to the

beach is only passable with an off-road vehicle. (Don't worry if you haven't got one, there are a number places to rent off-road vehicles in Jandía Playa.)

Playa de Barlovento

The tiny El Islote Peninsula is what separates Playa de Barlovento from Playa de Cofete. It is followed by 10 kilometers of completely deserted sandy beach – great hiking terrain, but without a trace of shade. There are hardly any facilities and you should avoid swimming here because of the fierce undertow! As the name Barlovento suggests, the wind always blows in from the sea. (It takes about one hour to walk from Cofete to the beginning of the beach at El Islote).

Playa del Viejo Rey

This beach of golden sand, below the steep coast near the vacation resort of La Pared, is in a beautiful location, and nearby there are other tiny coves sur-

rounded by countryside. Before swimming here you should always ask about the current conditions, since (especially during the winter) the undertow can be extremely dangerous.

Playa de Tarajalejo

This beach of coarse sand is about one kilometer long and is on the outskirts of the charming fishing village of Tarajalejo, on the southeastern coast. The further you get from the houses the quieter it is. Piles of lava rocks offer sun-worshippers some protection from the usually rather strong wind. Above the beach there is a narrow palm-lined pedestrian promenade and there are several bars and restaurants in Tarajalejo itself.

Playa de los Pobres

The somewhat secluded fishing village of Las Playitas still evokes the impression of how Fuerteventura might have looked in earlier times, before tourism became so

67

popular. The two-kilometer-long beach begins just south of the harbor and it is alternately covered by coarse sand and stones. It is safe for swimming and you are well protected from the wind. Large boulders provide shade in some places. Locals love to visit this beach, particularly on the weekends, while tourists are rarely seen. For the perfect ending to a perfect day you should try a seafood platter at one of the beach restaurants or at *Casa Victor* (address on page 45), which is, according to many, the very best fish restaurant on Fuerteventura.

Playa del Castillo

This semicircle of sandy beach, kilometers long, is located in the bay of the tourist resort of Caleta de Fustes. An offshore harbor jetty keeps the big waves at

Above: After going for a swim, explore the market in Cleta de Fustes (Playa del Castillo). Right: Refreshingly difficult for tourists to access – the quiet sandy beach near El Cotillo.

bay and the water is quite shallow, so don't hesitate to take even small children with you into the water. (This is why you will usually see and unusually high number of families.) The short and convenient pedestrian paths to the nearby Barceló Club are also quite family friendly. Several restaurants, bars and snack bars have been set-up near the harbor at the far northern end of Playa del Castillo. There is also a windsurfing and a diving school, both of which offer beginner lessons that are taught in this calm bay.

Playa de los Muertos

The somewhat strange name "beach of the dead" stems from the Middle Ages, when Jean de Béthencourt tried to conquer the island at this very place. He did not succeed, however, due to the fierce resistance of the Guanches. In remembrance of his numerous victims the beach is still referred to as Playa de los Muertos. This black sand and gravel beach is mainly frequented by locals who flock here with their picnic baskets on the weekends. While part of the family prepares the meal, the other tries its luck with the fishing pole. Since the surf can be very strong on some days, swimming is not always easy, yet the rolling, thundering waves quickly grab your attention with their spectacular and relentless pounding. And just in case you didn't bring a picnic with you, there are two restaurants directly on the beach that serve mouthwatering Canarian cuisine.

Playa Blanca

Puerto del Rosario's beach is located a few kilometers south of town. This beach of white sand is a popular destination with the locals, particularly on the weekends. It is also home to the capital's best hotel, the Parador Nacional de Fuerteventura. Located directly on the beach it and has one of the island's best restau-

rants as well as a picturesque courtyard and typical Canarian décor.

Caletillas de Castillo

North of El Cotillo you will find several little coves that are separated from each other by lava rocks. They are called *caletillas*. The tiny, nearly white, beaches (often just a few hundred meters in length) are relatively deserted, even though offshore lava rocks prevent breakers from reaching the beach. The natural contrast of the light-colored sand, black lava rocks and turquoise water is fascinating. Right near the beach is the restaurant *Azzurro*, the only building in the rather barren landscape. It has nice terrace where they serve fresh pasta and fish dishes.

Playa de Corralejo

Like a black line the asphalt road, shimmering in the heat, separates the almost endless Playa de Corralejo from the wide landscape of dunes. Near the two hotels you can rent deck chairs and sunshades. There are also a number of kiosks that sell beach paraphernalia, snacks and cold drinks nearby. On the beach itself there is hardly any shade, but you can always find plenty of secluded spots. Across the narrow strait of El Río, you can see Isla de los Lobos, but keep in mind that swimming here can be dangerous since there is a strong undertow in the channel.

Playa de la Calera

There is a marvelous swimming bay on Isla de los Lobos, just a few minutes away from the dock. Its crescent shape keeps any waves from rolling onto the beach and the water off the light-colored, sandy beach is quite shallow. This is an ideal place in which to relax in complete peace for several hours. Before returning to Corralejo you might take a little detour to one of the restaurants in the nearby fishing village El Puertito.

EXCURSION TO LANZAROTE

For a stunning view of Lanzarote, climb Montaña de Lobos, the highest peak on Isla de los Lobos, just north of Fuerteventura. On a clear day you can even see the outline, probably a bit fuzzy, of this neighbor island's coast. Above the coast you can make out Lanzarote's volcanic cones and can even tell that the color of the lava rocks are a lot darker than those on Fuerteventura. At night you can easily see the lights of the coastal resort of Playa Blanca in the distance.

Vacationers who are staying in Corralejo shouldn't miss the chance to visit Lanzarote, the nearest neighboring Canary Island, especially since the ferry connections between the two islands are particularly convenient.

The crossing only takes 35 minutes; including setting off and docking it will

Above: The "mountains of fire" on Lanzarote.
Right: Taking a break in a remote village – the people here always have time for a chat.

take you less than an hour to get from one island to the other. Vehicles, motorcycles and bicycles may be taken across, but in the case of rental cars you should check with the rental company to make sure your insurance covers such a crossing.

Once you arrive in Playa Blanca you will have to decide how you want to explore the island. You have a number of options.

By far the most comfortable way to explore Lanzarote is to take a bus tour that leads you past the island's various sights, one by one, and offers the added bonus of a guide.

Another possibility is to rent a car from one of the companies at the harbor or in Playa Blanca. This option makes you independent, of course, and allows you to see as much of Lanzarote and its sights as you would like to, at a pace you set yourself.

If you enjoy getting close to nature and are willing to restrict yourself to the southern end of the island, you can also choose to explore Lanzarote by bike.

Cycling in the South

If you want to explore Lanzarote by bike we recommend that you rent a bike from *España Bike* in **Playa Blanca**, near the left-hand side of the harbor. In addition to renting bikes, they also offer guided tours. If you decide to take a tour, Karin Harbsmeier, the friendly owner, will arrange to have you and your bike transported to the respective starting points. A mini-van accompanies each tour, carrying your belongings and allowing tired riders to hitch a ride.

If you prefer to set off on your own you should head out of town in a northerly direction. A narrow asphalted side road starts near the city limits and runs alongside the main road. It is rarely used and you won't have to worry about a lot traffic. The road leads through the Rubincón Plain, a barren landscape of reddish stones that have crystallized. Your first destination is *Yaiza, which is located in a valley between the Timanfaya volcano and the Ajaches Mountain Range.

Yazia has twice been selected as "the prettiest village in Spain." A slow ride through this peaceful town leads through narrow lanes that are lined by dazzlingly white houses. Green doors and window frames, together with lavishly planted front yards that are surrounded by low stone walls, are everywhere.

From Yaiza you have to backtrack a little before turning right and heading to *El Golfo. A short while later you will see a lava bed that is several kilometers in length and reaches right to the edge of the road. This barren volcanic landscape makes a much stronger impression when seen from a bike than from a car. At the crossroads leading to the village of El Golfo, on the right-hand side, keep to the left and circumnavigate the crescent-shaped remainder of a **crater** that faces the Atlantic. Set against the magnificent backdrop of this reddish-black semi-crater, the green saltwater lagoon of **Charco de los Clicos** sits in stark contrast to its black volcanic surroundings. The green color of this salty lagoon comes from a species of algae that makes the water impermeable to light.

Continue along the western coast in a southerly direction. Soon you will reach the two caves that are known as **Los Hervidores** (The name means "boiling/bubbling."). Below the cliffs the waves of the Atlantic constantly beat against the rocks, making an incessant noise.

The next sight is **Salinas de Janubio**, a former saltworks where up to 300,000 tons of "white gold" were once taken from the sea annually. Windmills pumped seawater into the shallow pools where it quickly evaporated in the heat of the sun, leaving behind the familiar coarse salt crystals. From here you can easily take the now-familiar side road back to Playa Blanca.

By Car to the Volcano

A visit to ****Parque Nacional de Timanfaya**, a massive volcanic plain that cover more than 50 square kilometers, will be among the highlights of your stay on the Canary Islands and your visit to Lanzarote. From Playa Blanca you can take a side road, via Yaiza, directly to the park, the boundaries of which are marked by little "fire flies" by the local artist César Manrique. From the park gates, where you have to pay an entrance fee, drive another two kilometers to the tourist center at **Montañas de Fuego**, the "mountains of fire." From there you can board any of the waiting buses and take the *Ruta de los Volcanes* tour (14-kilometer round-trip) through this unique volcanic landscape. Fields of giant chunks of lava alternate with mountains of fine lava ash. The colors here range from a light ochre to a reddish brown to a deep black. Along the way, the bus stops in a number of particularly interesting locations, allowing you to take some pictures. Unfortunately you are not allowed to get off the bus to explore this unique landscape on your own.

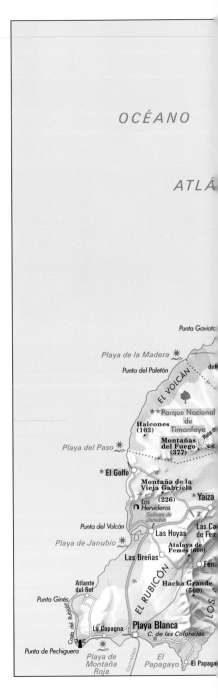

LANZAROTE

0   2,5   5 km

As soon as the bus returns to the tourist center, after no more than an hour, there are some interesting demonstrations about volcanoes. First, a park guide empties a bucket of water down a hole in the ground, which subsequently causes a mighty geyser of steam to hiss and shoot high into the sky – even at a depth of seven meters the temperature is higher than 350°C. After that, the guide puts some brushwood into a cave-like opening and it spontaneously catches fire just a few moments later.

If you feel hungry, why not have some chicken drumsticks at the nearby restaurant *El Diablo* where you meal is prepared in a very unique way? Beneath its large grill you won't find any charcoal – El Diablo grills everything using volcanic heat from the ground. It is hot enough to roast pieces of meat crispy brown in no time at all.

Above: Delicious food cooked over hellish heat at the El Diablo Restaurant. Right: The weird geometry of the vineyards in La Gería.

South of the entrance to the restaurant is a **camel station**. From here tourists can rock and roll a short distance through the volcanic landscape on the back of a dromedary.

If you want to continue adding to your knowledge of volcanoes after leaving the Timanfaya National Park, just head to the **Centro de Visitantes e Interpretación** (Visitors' Center) southwest of **Mancha Blanca**. Here you can look at several volcano-related exhibits and experience an audio-visual performance that offers even more insight into the world of volcanoes.

The next scenic highlight on your tour of Lanzarote is the wine-growing region of ****La Gería**. To either side of the small road from Uga (three kilometers east of Jaiza) to Mozaga, farmers have dug small funnel-shaped holes into and planted vines in the black volcanic ashes. At night the porous volcanic material absorbs dewdrops then feeds moisture to the vines during the day. The special character of the anthracite landscape, marked by these funnel-shaped openings (*zocos*), lead the

New York Museum of Modern Art to declare the entire region as belonging to the genre of "land art."

By the way, don't miss the opportunity to visit one of the numerous *bodegas* that are located throughout the heart of this wine-producing region. It is a perfect way to cap a day-trip to the island.

Highlights of the North

In contrast to Fuerteventura, distances are rather short on Lanzarote. In under an hour you can reach the north of the island from Playa Blanca by car. Drive to **Teguise** via Yaiza. From here go through the "Valley of 10,000 Palms" and on to ***Haría**, a town of just 2000 inhabitants, which, in view of the sparsely populated north, is still a considerable number. The facades of the village houses are well looked after and there are some really striking Andalusian-style townhouses with small wooden balconies. If you have the time, visit the **Museo Internacional de Miniaturas** and admire a curious

world in miniature format. The museum's displays range from delicately painted grains of rice to a miniature bible. In many cases you can't really appreciate these works without using a magnifying glass. Other displays include tiny reproductions of the works of César Manrique, the island's most famous son.

Just 10 kilometers outside Harí you approach the far northern tip of Lanzarote. The road leads just past the cliffs, affording one of the most exhilarating views of the entire Canarian archipelago. From ***Mirador del Río** (500 meters), which is impressivly located high on the mountainside, you can see the small islands of La Graciosa, Mantaña Clara and Alegranza just off the coast. Next to the viewing platform there is a restaurant. It was designed by the local artist César Manrique and in 1973 it was elaborately built into the rock. Here you can enjoy a cup of coffee and through the giant picture windows you can admire the fabulous view and gaze in amazement at the pink-colored salt garden below the observation

point. The remarkable colors of **Salinas del Río**, a disused saltworks, come from small crustaceans that live in the water of the saltpans.

The road then leads to **Órzola**. Ferries to the neighboring island of La Graciosa leave from its harbor three times a day. This is a good place to stop and enjoy a marvelous seafood platter at one of the many local restaurants.

From Órzola take the coastal road in the direction of Arrieta in order to reach two unique sights. **★Cueva de los Verdes** is a multi-story tunnel system that has emerged from a lava bed. Groups of visitors are taken through narrow tunnels, where taller visitors have to duck their heads, before going into the lava grottoes that extend up to 50 meters into the earth. Bizarre stone formations can be seen on the grottoes' walls and ceiling. Two hundred years ago Cueva de los Verdes was

Above: Uniquely styled interior architecture – subterranean living in a volcanic bubble à la César Manrique (Taro de Tahiche).

used as a hiding place by locals who were seeking shelter after spotting marauding pirates. The caves got their name from the Green (*Verde*) family who were among those who once hid here.

★★Los Jameos del Agua, which belongs to the same cave system, is also nearby. Here you descend a steep flight of stairs that leads to a subterranean saltwater lagoon where thousands of tiny albino crabs live. (Don't throw coins; corroding metals can poison the crabs.) In and around Los Jameos del Agua, César Manrique has created an unparalleled living space. Regardless of whether it is the shimmering turquoise of the swimming pool, the niches that have been artistically hewn out of the sheer rock or the large rooms in the adjacent "House of the Volcanoes," this visionary artist has, with a stroke of creative genius, managed to infuse this lava bubble with life.

The **Casa de los Volcanes** houses a volcanic studies center where the now-familiar subject of volcanic activity is again clearly documented.

The route now leads along the coast to **Arrieta** with its stunning beach. This small village also boasts a couple of fine restaurants, including *Miguel* with its terrace overlooking the sea.

Continue in a southerly direction and near the town of **Guatíza** you will find another of César Manrique's works of art: the spectacular arena-shaped **Jardín de Cactus** (cactus garden). It has been carefully modeled on a Japanese garden, right down to the smallest detail, a fact that makes a visit a must for everyone, not just fans of the prickly plant. Below a restored windmill you can see nearly 1500 different cactus species, the majority of them are indigenous to the Canary Islands.

The highlight for all Manrique fans, however, is a visit to the ****Fundación César Manrique** in **Tahiche**. In 1963, the artist had his house (1500 square meters) built here in the middle of black lava fields, inside five subterranean volcanic bubbles, according to his own specifications. He lived here until 1987. Just a short time before his tragic death in a car accident in September 1992, the necessary renovations were finished and the foundation was dedicated. It houses a majority of César Manrique's art works including his paintings, drawings, sketches, ceramics, photographs and numerous plans for both completed and non-completed projects. Even if you don't particularly care for Manrique's work, the Fundación is worth visiting just to see the amazingly luxurious and original setting, which has largely been left just as it was when it was his home.

To return to Playa Blanca you take the road to the island capital of **Arrecife** and continue along the highway until you get to the airport. From there a small side roads leads, via **Tias** and Yaiza, back to Playa Blanca. This drive will leave you with a lasting impression of Lanzarote's distinctive character and charm, and may inspire you to spend your next vacation on the "Isle of Volcanoes."

LANZAROTE

FERRY: **Naviera Armas** and **Líneas Fred Olsen** commute alternately. Departure times Corralejo/ Fuerteventura – Playa Blanca/Lanzarote: daily 8, 9, 10 & 11 am and 2, 5, 6, 7 & 8 pm; Playa Blanca – Corralejo: daily 7, 8, 9, 10 & 11 am and 2, 5, 6 & 7 pm; one-way ticket: adults 1800 ptas, children 900 ptas.

CUEVA DE LOS VERDES

Caves, tel: 928 173 220; daily 10 am-6 pm. Guided tours for groups of more than 20 people.

GUATIZA

Jardín de Cactus, tel: 928 529 397; daily 10 am-6 pm. Cafeteria, daily 11 am-4 pm.

HARÍA

Muséo Internacional de Miniaturas, Calle Palmeral 4, tel: 928 835 760; daily 10 am-6 pm.

LOS JAMEOS DEL AGUA

Cave System, created by C. Manrique, with bar, restaurant, shop, tel: 928 848 020; Tue, Fri & Sat. Folklore, daily 9:30 am-7 pm, 3 am when there are performances. Restaurant, 1-4 pm & 8-11:30 pm.

ÓRZOLA

Mirador del Río, panorama view; 10 am-6 pm.

PARQUE NACIONAL DE TIMANFAYA

Entrance fee incl. bus tour of the "fire mountains" (45 min, from Islote de Hilario); daily 9 am-4:45 pm. *CAMEL RIDING:* Echadero de los Camellos, on the road between Yaiza and Tinajo; daily 9 am-2 pm.

Restaurante El Diablo, Islote de Hilario, tel: 928 840 056/057; daily 9 am-3:30 pm. Meat & fish dishes grilled over a deep volcanic hole in the ground.

Museo de Rocas, Echadero de los Camellos, on the Yaiza–Tinajo road; Mon-Sat 9 am-2 pm; admission free. Exhibits about the national park.

Centro de Visitantes e Interpretación de Mancha Blanca (Visitor's Center), on the Yaiza–Tinajo road, tel/fax: 928 840 839; daily 9 am-5 pm; admission free. Film presentations 9 am-4 pm, on the hour. **Oficinas del Parque Nacional de Timanfaya**, Tinajo, Calle Laguneta 85, tel: 928 840 238/240, fax: 928 840 251; Mon-Fri 9 am-2 pm.

PLAYA BLANCA

España Bike Travel, Katrin Harbsmeier, Punta Limones 16, tel: 928 518 057. City and mountain bike rentals, guided tours with bus transfer.

TAHICHE

Fundación César Manrique, Taro de Tahiche, tel: 928 843 138/070; July-Oct: daily 10 am-7 pm; Nov-June: Mon-Sat 10 am-6 pm, Sun 10 am-3 pm.

UGA

Bodega El Chupadero, on the highway, 4 km north of Uga; Mon-Sat 10 am-8 pm.

CANARIAN CUISINE
Substantial and Delicious

The Canary Islands have been one of the most popular vacation destinations among Europeans for decades now, so it is no surprise to encounter dishes from all of the tourists' countries of origin when you go out to eat in the large resorts here. With all of the Irish pubs and German Bierkellers everywhere, it is hard to find anything authentically Canarian.

If you really want to get to know Canarian cuisine, you will need to head inland. Restaurants can be divided into three categories: simple, small ones with good home-style cooking; large places that are a popular destination by themselves, where local families take all of their relatives on the weekends, serve

Above: Mojo, a dip that comes in a number of variations, gofio and watercress soup are all important components of Canarian cooking. Right: Dried fish is often sold right in the harbor.

meat and seafood specialties; and rather expensive gourmet establishments where refined Canarian cuisine is served to those who can afford it.

Canarian cuisine originated as the rural cooking of the Spanish and Portuguese immigrants, flavored with Latin American influences. The wealthier households enjoyed produce grown on their own estates, or imported from overseas. Very filling meat dishes and sweet desserts were a regular feature of every main meal, and still are today. In the coastal towns seafood, simply but deliciously prepared in a variety of ways, was the main dish. Tenant farmers, day laborers and their wives often had to rely on *gofio* and potatoes as basic foodstuffs. *Gofio*, roasted flour made of wheat, maize or chickpeas, is one of the few foods still eaten today that dates back to the times of the Guanches.

Each household had (and still has) its own recipe for the typical Canarian sauce known as *mojo*, of which there are four basic types: a spicy mojo, with small red chili peppers marinated in olive oil and wine vinegar (*mojo picón* or *mojo rojo*); a green mojo with herbs (*mojo verde*); a garlic-dip mojo (*mojo de ajo*); and finally a saffron mojo with oregano and garlic (*mojo de azafrán*).

Tapas, those delicious Spanish appetizers, are available in almost all of the restaurants and bars on the islands. They can range from cheese with olives to ham, vegetables, fish and meat, all served in delicious sauces.

Thick Soups and Hearty Stews

Soup is often served before the main course. There are various kinds of fish soup, and also vegetable soups that are known as *potajes*, which are usually very thick because of their high potato content. Pumpkins, cabbages and beans are also popular ingredients. One popular "Soup of the Day" is *sopa de berros*, made from watercress. If you order a *sopa de garbanzos* (chickpea soup) you'd better be hungry because it is often as filling as an entire meal.

Stews play a great role in Canary Island cookery. A *puchero canario* contains up to seven different kinds of meat, all cooked with tomatoes, carrots, onions and chickpeas. In addition to those ingredients there is a broth that includes beans, white cabbage, yellow squash, sweet corn, sweet potatoes and taro root. To spice things up a bit the locals use crushed garlic cloves, pepper, cloves, oil, and – if you want a really filling meal – some salted meat and *chorizo,* a smoked red sausage. Sliced pears or other fruit may also be added.

Once your stew arrives, you first eat the meat and vegetables; then you take some *gofio* flour out of a bowl and roll it into balls before dipping it into whatever sauce you have left in your bowl – it is a delicious and very filling side dish. Whatever sauce is left behind after the *gofio* is gone is eaten with a spoon.

Canarian Cuisine

Other stews include *sancocho*, a simple vegetable stew that is usually livened up with pieces of meat or fish (usually dried fish), and *olla potrida*, which is almost always made with pieces of beef, sausage and vegetables.

Marinated Rabbit

It is virtually the Canarian national dish: marinated rabbit with boiled potatoes (*conejo en salmorejo con papas arrugadas*). The rabbit is left to marinate overnight (longer if possible) in a mixture of garlic, parsley, oregano, thyme, paprika, salt, pepper, oil and vinegar. Then it is slowly cooked and basted, and occasionally sprinkled with wine, in a ceramic pot until the flesh almost falls from the bones. Small, whole potatoes are served as a side dish. The potatoes, which are a common feature at almost any Canarian meal, are boiled in their skins in a pot of seawater until they crinkle up and get a shiny white crust of sea salt on the outside, which is not eaten.

Fresh Seafood

Delicious fresh fish is served in all of the local fishing villages, and in the best restaurants you can choose exactly with fish you want. The range on offer usually includes hake (*merluza*), angler (*sama*), sole (*lenguado*), sea bass (*mero*) and a kind of brace (*vieja*). On top of that, they have tuna steaks (*atún*), swordfish (*pez espada*) and shark (*tiburón*). Try the brace baked in salt, too (*dorada a la sal*).

If you aren't very hungry try the octopus (*pulpo*) and squid (*calamares*), served as *tapas*. From depths of up to 700 meters they catch shrimp (*cangrejos*), prawns (*gambas*) and lobster, including the elongated *langostas canarias*. If you

Above: Tuna – fresh from the boat. Right: Just one part of the ritual – checking a wine's color as a prelude to tasting. Following Pages: Fuerteventura's sparse vegetation should be treated with care, but that doesn't much bother the island's 40,000 goats, which out number the people!

are unfamiliar with dried cod (*bacalao*), only eat it if it is recommended.

Desserts

After the meal, before coffee and/or *coñac*, Canarios indulge in a sweet and usually high-calorie dessert (*postre*). The flambéed bananas are filling, as are *turrón de gofio*, an almond dessert made with honey, flour and figs, *bienmesabe*, a sweet dish made with eggs and almonds, and *frangollo*, which is made with maize and milk. Alternatively you can have a piece of fresh fruit.

Cheese

Smoked and unsmoked sheep and goat cheese is produced on all of the islands; it usually has a strong, slightly salty taste. The simple goat's cheese *queso blanco* is served almost everywhere. An island specialty is the mild cheese known as "flower cheese" (*queso de flor*) from Gran Canaria, produced in Guía from

fresh sheep and cow's milk. It gets its name from the bluish-purple artichoke flowers that are used in its production and can be found in three stages of ripeness: *tierno* (soft/young), *semicurado* (half-cured) and *viejo* (aged).

Drinks

The islands' mineral water (*agua mineral*) is good, and is either *con gas* or *sin gas* (carbonated or non-carbonated). Fruit juices (*zumos de fruta*) are usually freshly squeezed, and milkshakes (*batidos*) are mixed with ice cream or fruit. The light-green *batido de aguacate*, made with avocados, is very creamy.

For warmer temperatures, assuming it is enjoyed in moderation, the local beer (*cerveza*) is ideal; it comes in two brands, "Dorada" and "Tropical." At mealtimes, wines from Lanzarote and Tenerife are recommended; good-quality wines from the Spanish mainland are also available. There is a choice between *vino tinto* (red), *rosado* (rosé) and *blanco* (white).

Instead of a dessert wine with coffee after a meal, you can also try *ron miel*, a honey rum, or a banana liqueur (*crema de banana*). Restaurants attached to wine estates often serve *Aguardiente de Parra*, a clear spirit that is distilled on the premises.

If you feel like coffee after the meal, you can have a *café solo*, an ordinary small black espresso, or a *café doble*, which is the same thing but twice as big. If a little milk is added, it becomes a *café cortado*, which is far more popular with the locals than regular coffee with milk (*café con leche*). European-style filter coffee (*café alemán*) is also available in many places.

In the tourist centers, exotic cocktails are ubiquitous. Every known type – from Planter's Punches to Singapore Slings – are brought to your table with sparklers in to them. One simpler, yet equally good cocktail is a *Mojito Cubano*, made from a mixture of Havana rum and fresh mint, which was brought back from Cuba by returning emigrants.

METRIC CONVERSION

Metric Unit	US Equivalent
Meter (m)	39.37 in.
Kilometer (km)	0.6241 mi.
Square Meter (sq m)	10.76 sq. ft.
Hectare (ha)	2.471 acres
Square Kilometer (sq km)	0.386 sq. mi.
Kilogram (kg)	2.2 lbs.
Liter (l)	1.05 qt.

TRAVEL PREPARATIONS

Tourist Information

In the United Kingdom: Spanish Tourist Office, 57-58 St. James's Street, London SW1A 1LD, tel: 0171 499 0901. For brochures, tel: 0891 669 920.

In the United States: Tourist Offices of Spain, 665 Fifth Avenue, New York, NY 10022, tel: (212) 759-8822; 8383 Wiltshire Boulevard, Suite 960, Beverly Hills, CA 90211, tel: (213) 658-7188; Water Tower Place, Suite 915 East, 845 North Michigan Avenue, Chicago, IL 60611, tel: (312) 642-1992 and (312) 944-0216, fax: (312) 642-9817; 1221 Brickell Avenue, Miami, FL 33131, tel: (305) 358-1992, fax: (305) 358-8223.

In Canada: Spanish Tourist Office, 102 Bloor Street West, 14th Floor, Toronto, Ontario M5S 1M8, tel: (416) 961-3131 and 961-4079, fax: (416) 961-1992.

In Australia: Spanish Tourist Office, 203 Castlereagh Street, Level 2, Suite 21A, P.O. Box 675, 2000 Sydney, NSW, tel: 02 264 7966.

Internet Addresses

The following Internet addresses can be useful sources for additional information when you are planning a trip to Fuerteventura: http://gias720.dis.ulpgc.es, www.okspain.org, www.red2000.com, and www.abcanarias.com.

Spanish Embassies

UK: Spanish Embassy, 20 Peel Street, London W8 7PD, tel: 0171 727 2462 and 0171 243 8535, fax: 0171 229 4965.

US: Spanish Embassy, 2375 Pennsylvania Ave. NW, Washington DC 20037-1736, tel: (202) 728-2335, fax: (202) 728-2313.

Canada: Spanish Embassy, 74 Stanley Avenue, Ottawa, Ontario K1M 1P4, tel: (613) 747-2252, fax: (613) 744-1224.

Entry Regulations

Anyone planning to stay for up to three months will need to have a valid passport. Anyone planning to stay longer than three months should get a visa from the Spanish embassy or consulate in your native country.

Visa extensions while on the Canaries must be applied for at the *Gobierno Civil* in Santa Cruz de Tenerife or Las Palmas de Gran Canaria. An application certification from the consulate of your own country is needed for this, along with an application certificate for the municipality in which you intend to reside. In addition, you must show proof that you have health insurance. In certain cases an adequate income must also be proven by bank guarantee.

Anyone arriving in their own car, by ferry, needs to have a green international insurance card, as well as the registration usual papers and a driver's license.

For pets, such as cats and dogs, an official veterinary certificate, which may not be more than two weeks old, must be presented. It must confirm in both English and Spanish that the animal has been vaccinated against rabies within the past year, and at least one month before entry.

Health

The same health guidelines apply to the Canary Islands that apply to the rest of Europe. This includes considering vaccinations against tetanus and polio. And, of course, condoms should always be used to minimize the risk of contracting AIDS, known as SIDA in Spanish.

There are good pharmacies almost everywhere on the islands and they sell many common medications, even though they may have different names. If you bring along the paper that is normally enclosed with medications, or a at least a description of the medication from your physician, the Spanish pharmacist can generally figure out what it is that you need and provide you with the Spanish equivalent.

Pharmacies can be recognized by the green or red Maltese crosses on the sign outside, and in the cities and larger towns there is always at least one emergency pharmacy that is open all night long (see also "Medical Treatment / Pharmacies," on pages 89-90).

Under EU regulations, an E111 form should cover medical treatment for residents of Great Britain while on Fuerteventura. This can often lead to delays and red tape, however, so it is best to have your own private insurance if possible. American visitors should also check that their health insurance provides them with adequate coverage, and take out an additional travel insurance policy if necessary.

The standard of health care in the hospitals here is first class, and many towns also have a facility that can provide first aid or emergency treatment. Most doctors speak good English.

Ambulances will take you to the nearest available hospital, which will treat your complaint, but many are private and will only treat you if you have private medical insurance – so it's very important to have the relevant documents.

Clothing

For a pure beach holiday you'll be fine with just light summer clothing in both summer and winter; warmer clothing is only needed in the evenings, or if wind is strong. Despite the mild temperatures on Fuerteventura, you should not underestimate the power of the sun – good sun protection is essential, especially on windy days.

Even though casual clothing is usually okay, the better hotels on the island consider etiquette important at mealtimes, and especially in the evenings, when more formal clothing is required; the same applies to expensive restaurants and cultural events.

Those who have chosen accommodation at higher altitudes (from 500 meters to over 1500 meters), or are planning to hiking in the mountains, should expect repeated rain showers and cooler temperatures (up to 10°C cooler than on the coast). Bring along rain protection, a light sweater or jacket, and sturdy shoes for unpaved paths.

When to Go

Fuerteventura is a popular travel destination all year round. The peak season is during European vacation times, in the fall, at Christmas and during carnival and Easter, and flights and accommodation have to be booked well in advance, often up to six months before your trip. In the winter a lot of retirees come here to stay warm, while in the summer you are more likely to meet young and middle-aged people.

Currency Exchange / Regulations

Until it gives way to the Euro, the Spanish peseta (abbreviated "Pta") is the country's unit of currency. There are 20,000, 10,000, 5,000, 2,000 and 1,000 Pta banknotes; 500, 200, 100, 50, 25, 10, 5, 2 and 1 Pta coins. The 5-Pta coin commonly known as a *duro*.

The current exchange rate is:

US $1 . . . . 174 Ptas
UK £1 . . . . 278 Ptas
AUS $1. . . . . 106 Ptas

Incidentally, a little sound financial advice: Only exchange a small amount of pesetas at home, enough to cover things you until you can get to a local bank, because the exchange rate on the island is usually a lot better. Any amount of foreign currency can be brought with you to Fuerteventura. If you want to take out large sums of money, it is best to declare it – because the maximum permissible amount per person without declaration is up to one million pesetas and foreign currency with an equivalent value of 500,000 Ptas.

There are cash machines in all of the island's holiday resorts and large towns. Traveler's checks, cash and Eurochecks can be exchanged for pesetas at any bank. Credit cards are accepted nearly everywhere (see also "Banks," on page 88).

ARRIVAL

By Plane

A lot of European charter flights go directly to the Fuerteventura. Tenerife and Gran Canaria are also served by larger European airlines, such as British Airways, Air France, Iberia, Lufthansa, Swissair, etc.

In general, package tours are cheaper than vacations that are tailored to your own preferences, which means comparing prices and offers by various travel agents is always a good idea. Most charter flights allow 20 kilograms of luggage, though if you're planning to stay longer you can apply to have the amount increased.

Special luggage (such as sports equipment) should be reported to the airline in advance; transporting a bicycle or surfboard usually costs around US $50-75 extra. If you want to take your pets along (in special containers), they must also be reported in advance. The price of their passage is based on their weight.

Passport checks are quite rare within the EU, which saves a lot of time and hassle, and luggage is only examined in special cases (suspected weapons or drugs, etc.). The entire customs and immigration procedure is a lot stricter for intercontinental flights.

In the arrivals hall you will find rental car companies, cash machines, tourist information, a post office and a currency exchange outlet.

Just after your arrival at the airport is a good time to exchange your currency for pesetas – you might be surprised at how favorable the rates are.

By Ship

A *Companía Trasmediterránea* ferry from Cádiz (on mainland Spain) stops in Santa Cruz de Tenerife and Las Palmas de Gran Canaria every Saturday. The trip takes around 40 or 48 hours, depending on where you disembark. From either city you can, Monday through Saturday, catch a *Jetfoil* high-speed catamaran to Morro Jable, on the Jandía Peninsula (3.5 or 1.5 hours, depending on your point of departure).

A car ferry travels between Las Palmas and Puerto del Rosario three times a week (8 hours). In the summer you have to book months in advance, mainly because of the relative lack of transportation capacity for automobiles.

Timetables, prices and applications can be obtained from **Companía Transmediterránea**, Plaza Manuel Gómez Moreno, E-28020 Madrid, Spain, tel: +(07) 914 238 500/832. Branch office: Avda. Ramón de Carranza 26/7, E-11006 Cádiz, Spain, tel: +(07) 956 287 850.

ISLAND-HOPPING

By Plane

Flights run by Iberia and its subsidiaries, or by other private firms, travel between the islands several times a day, and no flight takes longer than one hour. These flights can be booked at travel agencies at home, at the agencies in the Canary Islands themselves, from Iberia (also for its subsidiaries) or directly at the airports.

By Ship

In the Canary Islands the cheapest way to get from Point A to Point B is to "island-hop" by ferry. All of the islands are connected by car ferry, though not always directly. Gran Canaria and Fuerteventura, are also served by *Jetfoils*, high-speed catamarans (see page 86), but they are sensitive to choppy seas and don't always run.

Competing for ferry traffic are the state-run *Companía Trasmediterránea* (Las Palmas de Gran Canaria, tel: 928 260 070; see page 86), its subsidiary *Naviera Armas* (Las Palmas de Gran Canaria, tel: 928 474 080) and the private shipping company *Líneas Fred Olsen* (Santa Cruz de Tenerife, tel: 922 628 200). The price differences between all three are minimal. Tickets can be booked via travel agencies or at the companies' respective harbor offices. Tickets are usually still available just before departure, except on public holidays, so booking ahead isn't always necessary.

TRAVELING AROUND FUERTEVENTURA

By Bus

The island has an efficient public bus service network. Larger towns are served several times a day, but small villages aren't always part of the network (see the *INFO* section on pages 43-45).

Timetables are available at larger bus stations, near tourist offices, at the airports or in the vacation resorts. Group tickets and multiple-journey tickets care often be a lot cheaper than the usual rate.

By Taxi

Taxis are relatively inexpensive, but it is always best to settle on a price with the driver before the taxi actually starts to move. For overland trips it is a good idea to ask for a look at the list of fixed tariffs. As a rule, one kilometer costs 100 pesetas, but short trips they can be a bit more

expensive. There is also an official surcharge for trips on Sundays and public holidays.

By Rental Car

Economy class rental cars usually cost between 2200 and 2500 pesetas a day when you rent for at least a week, plus insurance of around 1200 pesetas a day. If you are staying longer you can generally negotiate a better rate.

The international car rental companies will reserve a car for you before you leave on vacation, but it is also possible to take advantage of local competitiveness and negotiate a deal with the smaller companies once your are on Fuerteventura. If you do find a cheap offer, make sure the vehicle is roadworthy, and also check the size of the rental fleet – so you don't have to waste two valuable days of your vacation waiting for a substitute vehicle that never appears.

You don't need to worry about getting an international driver's license, a national one is sufficient for renting a car. There is often a clause in the contract that says the driver has to be at least 21 years old. If you want others to be able to drive the car, their names must be in the contract and their driver's licenses shown.

Hitchhiking

On the island the locals hitchhike quite a lot, but that is usually because they know the drivers who are passing them. Tourists generally have a much harder time thumbing a ride.

Traffic Regulations

The traffic regulations are basically the same as the rest of Europe. Cars drive on the right, and seat belts must be fastened, even in town traffic. The alcohol limit is 0.8 – and police checks are particularly frequent late at night whenever there is a fiesta. NOTE: At traffic circles, unless otherwise indicated, vehicles that are entering the circle have the right-of-way.

If you suddenly have to slow down or stop because of an obstacle in the road, you can warn the driver behind by switching on your left indicator or sticking your left hand out of the window. On winding mountain roads it's always best to sound the horn before a sharp curve.

In the Canary Islands the speed limit in built-up areas is 60 km/h, on country roads 90 km/h, on major roads 100 km/h and on highways 120 km/h. On weekends some people tend to travel amazingly fast, and enjoy passing on bends, but most of the local drivers are generally very courteous and obliging.

PRACTICAL TIPS FROM A TO Z

Accommodation

Most accommodation is geared towards package tours; individual travelers who haven't booked in advance will find it difficult to find suitable and inexpensive accommodation in the tourist centers during peak season. Tourist information offices provide lists with prices and descriptions.

The Spanish authorities have divided hotels, boarding houses and apartments into categories. However, these only apply to furnishings, so the number of stars or key symbols an establishment may have says nothing about the actual quality of the service and the atmosphere there.

The official categories for hotels range from luxury (5-star) to simple (1-star); for apartments from high-class (3-star) to simple (1-star), and for boarding houses from pleasant family-run establishments (2-star) to very simple places (1-star) with shared showers and lavatories.

The categories in the *INFO* section on pages 43-45 have attempted to take atmosphere and service into account as well. Prices are based on the following scale: ☺ Budget: Double rooms up to 5000 pesetas. ☺☺ Moderate: Double rooms from 5000 to 10,000 pesetas. ☺☺☺ Luxury: Double rooms over 10,000 pesetas.

If you are interested in vacationing in a **Finca** (a country farmhouse, often recently renovated), your local travel agency at home or one of the offices on Fuerteventura can provide you with more details. The EU project *Turismo Rural*, whereby old buildings are being renovated and turned into vacation homes, offers a good selection.

Camping is not very widespread on Fuerteventura. Some beaches have become unofficial campsites, but this is just a tolerated exception to the rule. Communal or private campsites outside the nature reserves are rare, and are usually not very peaceful. Camping without a permit is forbidden inside the nature reserves, and even at the official locations you still have to get a permit in advance from the environmental or national park authorities (tourist offices can provide you with more information on this). It is worth making the extra effort to get the permit, however, because of the beauty of the sites. You should never camp in narrow ravines (*barrancos*) – they are prone to falling rocks and boulders!

Banks

Banks are open Monday through Friday from 9 a.m. to 2 p.m., Saturdays to 1 p.m., and slightly longer in the summer and during carnival. If you want to exchange cash or traveler's checks (there is a limit of 25,000 pesetas per check), remember that rates and commissions vary from bank to bank. Exchange outlets and hotels (unfavorable rates!) will change money and checks outside banking hours. Credit cards are accepted almost everywhere, cash machines are also a common sight (see "Currency Exchange / Regulations," on pages 85-86). Block lost checks or credit card immediately!

Crime

The Canary Islands are generally regarded as being relatively safe. Violent crime is rare, but petty crime does exist, especially on the large islands with all the tourism, urban poverty and drug problems. If you leave your car parked in a remote location, make sure you take all of the valuables out – and leave the glove compartment open so that it is clear that the car has nothing inside. Deposit your valuables in the hotel safe, especially in vacation villages. Also beware of free trips to buy cheap goods. If you agree to one of these, make sure you can assess the quality of what you're offered and check whether it might not be cheaper at home. The best-case scenario here is usually the loss of one day's vacation. If you get taken to a time-sharing location, don't sign anything resembling a contract. Legitimate firms allow people plenty of time to consider the whole thing, and provide access to experts and legal advisers.

On some very busy promenades you may get tricked out of your cash by professional tricksters (e.g., shell games) who are working together with seemingly uninvolved bystanders.

Customs Regulations

As long as the Canary Islands are not fully integrated into the EU, the customs regulations for entrance into the EU are the same for those of a non-EU state: the duty-free allowances are 200 cigarettes (or 250 grams of tobacco or 100 cigarillos or 50 cigars), one liter of spirits, and two liters of wine.

Once the islands have been fully integrated into the EU, and assuming no special regulations apply, the duty-free limit for import into an EU country will be 800 cigarettes (or 400 cigarillos or 200 cigars) and 90 liters of wine (or 10 liters of spirits or 20 liters of liqueur).

Disabled Assistance

The *Fundación OID* (*Organización Impulsora de Discapacitados*) provides help and information for the disabled. Their central office for the eastern province of the Canary Islands is located in Las Palmas de Gran Canaria, at Calle Manuel González Martín 22, tel: 928 292 315.

Electricity

The tourist centers have the two round pin sockets that are also the standard in France and Germany, so bring an adapter. The current is 220 volts. Some places still have 110 to 125 volts AC with sockets that need an extra adapter, too.

Emergencies

The emergency number to call on Fuerteventura is 092. For first aid or a medic, call 061. The number for the fire department is 080.

Gratuities

In bars and restaurants service is generally included in the bill, but good service is generally rewarded with a gratuity of around 10 percent of the bill. In hotels, chambermaids and porters are given a suitable amount on arrival and departure, especially if they clearly go out of their way to assist. Cab drivers expect around 10 percent of the fare. Outside the tourist centers, people are more ready to help without shooting calculating glances at your wallet.

Medical Treatment / Pharmacies

Medical treatment on the island is good almost everywhere. The hospitals are of European standards. Hotel receptions, tour operators or your consulate will give you the location of the nearest emergency room or medical practice. Many towns and even some small villages have first aid clinics that are operated by the Red Cross (*Cruz Roja*).

Pharmacies (*farmacias*; normally with a green or red Maltese cross on the sign), are open Monday through Friday from 9 a.m. to 1 p.m. and 4 to 8 p.m., and Saturdays from 9 a.m. to 1 p.m. Pharmacies in every large town have night and emergency opening hours (*Farmacia de*

Guardia). The signs outside them tell you which one is currently open, but after 10 p.m. you must have a prescription.

Thanks to good hygiene conditions, visitors hardly ever get sick. The most common ailments are caused by the change in climate and in diet. Give your body some time to adapt – avoid overdoing things on day one, eat food that is easily digestible, and drink lots of liquids, but not too much alcohol (if at all). Avoid long periods in the sun without proper protection. Tap water is clean and you can brush your teeth with it without worry (see also "Health," on pages 84-85).

Opening Hours

There are no firmly fixed opening times for businesses. Most stores are open Monday through Friday from 9 a.m. to 1 p.m. and 4:30 to 7:30 p.m., and Saturdays from 9 a.m. to 2 p.m. In the vacation resorts these times are more flexible depending on the season and the amount of business, and some stores are even open on Sundays.

Photography

A large selection of film material is available in the tourist centers, but it is rather more expensive than in other parts of Europe or the U.S. Always check the "sell-by" date. Film can be developed overnight in the tourist centers, and the prices are moderate.

Post Offices (Correo)

Generally speaking, the post offices offer all services, including poste restante, from Monday through Saturday (9 a.m. to 1 p.m.). In the big towns the main post offices are also open in the afternoons, and some don't even break for lunch.

Stamps for normal letters and postcards cost 65 pesetas for EU countries, 75 pesetas for non-EU European countries, and 95 pesetas for overseas destinations. Stamps can also be purchased at tobacconists, souvenir stores and hotels.

Public Holidays

The following are official public holidays in the Canary Islands:

January 1: New Year's Day (*Año Nuevo*).

January 6: Epiphany (*Los Reyes*).

March 19: St. Joseph's Day (*San José*).

May 1: Labor Day (*Día del Trabajo*).

May 30: Canaries Day (*Día de Canarias*).

July 25: St. Jacob's Day (*Santiago*).

August 15: Assumption Day (*Asunción*).

October 12: Day of the Spanish-Speaking World (*Día de la Hispanidad*).

November 1: All Saints' Day (*Todos los Santos*).

December 6: Constitution Day (*Día de la Constitución*).

December 8: Immaculate Conception (*Immaculada Concepción*).

December 25: Christmas (*Navidad*).

Moveable Holidays: Maundy Thursday, Good Friday, Easter, Whitsun, Ascension Day and Corpus Christi. Easter Monday, Whit Monday and Boxing Day are not public holidays in Spain.

The tourist offices on Fuerteventura can provide you with more detailed information about local religious festivals, pilgrimages and carnivals.

Swimming / Nude Sunbathing

Swimming in lonely bays without supervision can be very dangerous because of the powerful undertow and often sharp rocks. The surf can be tricky, especially on the windward side of the island. On beaches where there is supervision, signal flags tell you whether swimming is currently forbidden (red flag), only recommended for experienced swimmers (yellow flag) or allowed for everyone (green flag). Especially clean beaches also fly blue EU flags.

You will need to wear beach sandals in the black sand here, because it gets very hot – sandals are also useful as protection against sharp stones when you are in the water. Sun protection is absolutely essential, even if you aren't sunbathing! You should always wear sunscreen and a hat.

In most tourist centers, topless bathing has become a regular feature on the beach and by the pool. Nude sunbathing is severely frowned upon, however, and is only tolerated on secluded beaches, like the Las Dunas de Corralejo.

Telecommunications

You can dial abroad directly from phone booths bearing the words *internacional* or *interurbana*, either with coins or with phone cards. The latter, known as *tarjetas telefónicas*, are sold in 1000 and 2000 peseta versions at post offices, kiosks and souvenir stores. In the tourist centers you can also make phone calls from public phone offices (*teléfonos publicos*) without using coins. The number of units is simply added up at the end of the call.

The code for dialing abroad from Spain is 07. After you hear a beep, dial the country code followed by the area code (minus the initial zero if there is one), then the phone number itself.

No code is needed for calls within the island. The previous code, 928, is now a fixed part of the number.

National directory assistance can be reached at 003, and international information at 025. From Europe to the Canaries you dial 0034 for Spain and then the number. From outside Europe dial the international access code +(34) and the number.

Time

The time on Fuerteventura is the same as that in the U.K., i.e., Greenwich Mean Time, or one hour behind Central European Time. It also changes over to summer time – so there is no need for visitors from the U.K. to adjust their watches. Visitors from North America will need to change their watches between five and eight hours ahead, depending on their home time zone.

PHRASEBOOK

The official language on the Canary Islands is Spanish. In the tourist centers most people understand English pretty well, but a basic knowledge of Spanish is useful if you travel inland.

All words ending with a vowel, an "s" or an "n" and without any accent, always have their penultimate syllable stressed. All other words are either stressed on the syllable with the accent or – if there isn't an accent – on the last syllable. For instance, *Los Cristianos* = los cristiA̱nos; *El Escobonal* = el escobonA̱l; *Andén Verde* = andE̱n vE̱rde. Syllables with non-accented diphthongs count as one syllable, e.g., *Antigua* = antI̱gua; but: *Garafía* = garafI̱a.

Guidelines

Good morning . . . . . . *Buenos días*
Good afternoon . . . . . *Buenas tardes*
Good evening (early evening). . *Buenas tardes*
Good night . . . . *Buenas noches*
Hello! (between friends). . . . . *¡Hola!*
Goodbye . . . . *Hasta la vista*
Bye . . . . *Adiós*
See you later . . . . *Hasta luego*
See you tomorrow . . . . *Hasta mañana*
How are you?. . . . . *¿Qué tal?*
Thanks a lot . . . . . . *Muchas gracias*
Not at all . . . . *De nada*
Please . . . . *Por favor*
Go ahead . . . . *Sirvase Usted*
Excuse me . . . . *Perdón*
Yes . . . . *Sí*
No . . . . *No*
Do you speak English?. . *¿Habla Usted inglés?*
I don't understand Spanish . . . . . *No entiendo español*
Speak more slowly please . . . *Un poco mas despacio, por favor*
What's your name? . . *¿Cómo se llama Usted?*
My name is ... . *Me llamo ...*
I live in .... *Vivo en ...*
(Very) good . . . . *(Muy) bien*

Help! . . . . *¡Socorro!*
Turn left . . . . *A la izquierda*
Turn right . . . . *A la derecha*
Keep straight on. . . . *Siempre derecho*
How far is that?. *¿A qué distancia está?*
What time is it? . . . . . *¿Qué hora es?*
Up . . . . *Arriba*
Down . . . . *Abajo*
Here . . . . *Aquí*
There . . . . *Allí*
Who?. . . . . *¿Quién?*
Where? . . . . *¿Dónde?*
Where to? . . . . *¿Adonde?*
When? . . . . *¿Cuándo?*
How much?. . . . . *¿Cuánto?*
Where can I get ...? . . *¿Dónde hay ...?*
What does that cost? . . . *¿Cuánto vale
esto? ¿Cuanto cuesta?*
The menu please! . . . . . . *¡La lista de
platos! ¡El menú, por favor!*
The bill please! . *¡La cuenta, por favor!*
Do you have a room free? . . . . *¿Tiene
Usted una habitación libre?*
Double Room. . . . *Habitación doble*
Single Room. . . *Habitación individual*
For one night . . . . . . *Para una noche*
For one week . . . . . *Para una semana*
Can I see the room? . . . *¿Puedo ver la
habitación?*
I want to rent a car. . . . . . . *Quisiera
alquilar un coche*
I want to rent a boat . . . . . . *Quisiera
alquilar una barca*
Yesterday. . . . . *Ayer*
Today. . . . . *Hoy*
Tomorrow . . . . *Mañana*
Last night . . . . *Anoche*
Day after tomorrow . . *Pasado mañana*
Day before yesterday . . . . . *Anteayer*
Holiday . . . . *Día festivo*

Days of the Week

Monday. . . . . *Lunes*
Tuesday . . . . *Martes*
Wednesday . . . . *Miércoles*
Thursday . . . . *Jueves*
Friday . . . . *Viernes*
Saturday. . . . . *Sábado*
Sunday . . . . *Domingo*

Months

January . . . . *Enero*
February . . . . *Febrero*
March . . . . *Marzo*
April. . . . . *Abril*
May . . . . *Mayo*
June . . . . *Junio*
July . . . . *Julio*
August . . . . *Agosto*
September . . . . *Setiembre*
October. . . . . *Octubre*
November . . . . *Noviembre*
December . . . . *Diciembre*

In a Restaurant

Today's menu . . . . . . *Menú del día*
Dessert . . . . *Postre*
Bread . . . . *Pan*
Drink . . . . *Bebida*
Wine . . . . *Vino*
Beer . . . . *Cerveza*
Mineral water. . . . . . *Agua mineral*
Carbonated/uncarbonated . *Con/sin gas*
Black coffee. . . . . *Café solo*
Coffee with a little milk. . *Café cortado*
Milk coffee . . . . . . *Café con leche*
Breakfast . . . . *Desayuno*
Lunch . . . . *Almuerzo*
Supper . . . . *Cena*
Omelette . . . . *Tortilla*
Potato omelette. . . . *Tortilla Española*
Soup . . . . *Sopa*
Meat . . . . *Carne*
Beef . . . . *Carne de Vaca*
Pork. . . . . *Cerdo*
Veal . . . . *Ternera*
Chicken . . . . *Pollo*
Lamb . . . . *Cordero*
Fried . . . . *Frito*
Grilled . . . . *A la plancha*
Baked. . . . . *Asado*
Salad . . . . *Ensalada*
Vegetables . . . . *Verdura*
Peas and beans . . . . . . *Legumbres*
Fish. . . . . *Pescado*
Sea pike . . . . *Merluza*
Trout. . . . . *Trucha*
Salmon . . . . *Salmón*
Tuna . . . . *Atún*

Swordfish . . . . *Pez espada*
Squid . . . . *Calamares*
Octopus . . . . *Pulpo*

Numbers

0	*cero*
1	*un(o), una*
2	*dos*
3	*tres*
4	*cuatro*
5	*cinco*
6	*seis*
7	*siete*
8	*ocho*
9	*nueve*
10	*diez*
11	*once*
12	*doce*
13	*trece*
14	*catorce*
15	*quince*
16	*dieciséis*
17	*diecisiete*
18	*dieciocho*
19	*diecinueve*
20	*veinte*
21	*veintiún(o/a)*
22	*veintidós*
30	*treinta*
31	*treinta y uno*
100	*cien(to)*
101	*ciento uno*
200	*doscientos/-as*
300	*trescientos/-as*
1,000	*mil*
2,000	*dos mil*
3,000	*tres mil*
10,000	*diez mil*
100,000	*cien mil*
500,000	*quinientos mil*
1,000,000	*un millón (de)*

AUTHORS

Bernd F. Gruschwitz is a historian and Anglicist, and lives in Bremen, Germany. He has been a regular visitor to the Canary Islands since 1986, as a photographer and travel guide author. For this book he wrote the chapters "Fuerteventura – Sun, Sand, Wind and Stars" and "Canarian Cuisine." For Nelles Verlag he has also worked as an author and photographer on *Nelles Guide Bali/Lombok* and *Nelles Guide Prague*.

Wolfgang Taschner is a specialized freelance journalist and computer book publisher, as well as a travel guide author. He generally focuses his travel writings on the field of active nature holidays. He has written numerous books on the Canary Islands, which are among his favorite travel destinations. As co-author of this book he expanded the "Fuerteventura" chapter, and wrote the "Historical Overview" and several of the feature articles, including "The Windmill Route" and "Excursion to Lanzarote."

PHOTOGRAPHERS

Amberg, Gunda   cover, 25, 60, 64
Archiv für Kunst und Geschichte,
  Berlin   8
Bersick, Dr. Gerhard   22, 70
Bildagentur Dr. Wagner (Silvestris) 39
Eisenschink, Gerhard   71
Gruschwitz, Bernd   9, 14, 26, 30, 49,
              57, 69, 76, 78, 79, 80
Hackenberg, Rainer   3, 12/13, 20, 23,
          28, 32, 34, 36, 37, 38, 41, 48,
          54, 55, 58, 65, 68, 82/83
Heine, Heiner (Silvestris)   10/11, 18,
              21, 24, 27, 46/47, 51
Mitteregger, Chr. (Archiv Amberg) 67
Rausch, Simon (Silvestris)   61
Rostiti, Riccardo   29, 74
Scholten, Jo   81
Schulte, Wolfgang (Silvestris)   53
Stadler, Hubert   75
Stankiewitz, Thomas   31, 35, 40
Stuhler, Werner   33
Taschner, Wolfgang   50, 59, 62, 63
Thiele, Klaus   42
Thomas, Martin   19.

Guidelines

INDEX

Explore the World

NELLES MAPS

AVAILABLE TITELS

Afghanistan 1 : 1 500 000
Argentina *(Northern),* **Uruguay**
  1 : 2 500 000
Argentina *(Southern),* **Uruguay**
  1 : 2 500 000
Australia 1 : 4 000 000
Bangkok *- and Greater Bangkok*
  1 : 75 000 / 1 : 15 000
Burma → *Myanmar*
Caribbean - **Bermuda, Bahamas,
  Greater Antilles** 1 : 2 500 000
Caribbean - **Lesser Antilles**
  1 : 2 500 000
Central America 1 : 1 750 000
Central Asia 1 : 1 750 000
China *- Northeastern*
  1 : 1 500 000
China *- Northern* 1 : 1 500 000
China *- Central* 1 : 1 500 000
China *- Southern* 1 : 1 500 000
Colombia - Ecuador 1 : 2 500 000
Crete *-* Kreta 1 : 200 000
Dominican Republic - Haiti
  1 : 600 000
Egypt 1 : 2 500 000 / 1 : 750 000
Hawaiian Islands
  1 : 330 000 / 1 : 125 000
Hawaiian Islands – **Kauaʻi**
  1 : 150 000 / 1 : 35 000

Hawaiian Islands – **Honolulu
  - Oʻahu** 1 : 35 000 / 1 : 150 000
Hawaiian Islands – **Maui - Molokaʻi
  - Lānaʻi** 1 : 150 000 / 1 : 35 000
Hawaiian Islands – **Hawaiʻi, The Big
  Island** 1 : 330 000 / 1 : 125 000
Himalaya 1 : 1 500 000
Hong Kong 1 : 22 500
Indian Subcontinent 1 : 4 000 000
India *- Northern* 1 : 1 500 000
India *- Western* 1 : 1 500 000
India *- Eastern* 1 : 1 500 000
India *- Southern* 1 : 1 500 000
India *- Northeastern - Bangladesh*
  1 : 1 500 000
Indonesia 1 : 4 000 000
Indonesia **Sumatra** 1 : 1 500 000
Indonesia **Java - Nusa Tenggara**
  1 : 1 500 000
Indonesia **Bali - Lombok**
  1 : 180 000
Indonesia **Kalimantan**
  1 : 1 500 000
Indonesia **Java - Bali** 1 : 650 000
Indonesia **Sulawesi** 1 : 1 500 000
Indonesia **Irian Jaya - Maluku**
  1 : 1 500 000
Jakarta 1 : 22 500
Japan 1 : 1 500 000
Kenya 1 : 1 100 000
Korea 1 : 1 500 000

Malaysia 1 : 1 500 000
West Malaysia 1 : 650 000
Manila 1 : 17 500
Mexico 1 : 2 500 000
Myanmar *(Burma)* 1 : 1 500 000
Nepal 1 : 500 000 / 1 : 1 500 000
Nepal Trekking **Khumbu Himal -
  Solu Khumbu** 1 : 75 000
New Zealand 1 : 1 250 000
Pakistan 1 : 1 500 000
Peru - Ecuador 1 : 2 500 000
Philippines 1 : 1 500 000
Singapore 1 : 22 500
Southeast Asia 1 : 4 000 000
South Pacific Islands 1 : 13 000 000
Sri Lanka 1 : 450 000
Taiwan 1 : 400 000
Tanzania *-* Rwanda, Burundi
  1 : 1 500 000
Thailand 1 : 1 500 000
Uganda 1 : 700 000
Venezuela *-* Guyana, Suriname,
  French Guiana 1 : 2 500 000
Vietnam, Laos, Cambodia
  1 : 1 500 000

FORTHCOMING

Bolivia, Paraguay 1 : 2 500 000
Chile 1 : 2 500 000
Cuba 1 : 775 000

Nelles Maps are top quality cartography!
Relief mapping, kilometer charts and tourist attractions.
Always up-to-date!